SELL YOURSELF RICH

SELL YOURSELF RICH

G. WORTHINGTON HIPPLE

Foreword by
ARTHUR H. "RED" MOTLEY
Chairman of the Board of Parade Publications and formerly
President of the Chamber of Commerce of the United States.

acropolis
PERSONAL
Enrichment Series

ACROPOLIS BOOKS LTD. • WASHINGTON, D.C. 20009

THE ACROPOLIS PERSONAL ENRICHMENT SERIES

How To Make A Habit of Success	Inner Companions
Sell Yourself Rich	The Warm World of Martin Buxbaum
Law For The Layman	Tightening the Circle Over Eel Country
Strategies and Tactics for Getting a Government Job	Sonnets of Eve
Right First Job For You	Seeing in the Dark
Wall Street: Security Risk	So What Happened to You?
Dangers to Children and Youth	To the Water's Edge
The Shopper's Guidebook	Sue and Mindy Find a New Friend
How the Professional Can Make Money Outside His Profession	Matu and Matsue
Build Family Finances and Reduce Risks and Taxes	Uwharrie Magic
Save Your Health and Your Money	A Gallery of Children
How to Travel the World and Stay Healthy	The Ageless Story of Jesus
Pacific Paradise on a Low Budget	Tennis for Everyone
Historic Architecture of the U.S. Virgin Islands	A Trip Into Your Unconscious
Bottoms Up With a Rear Admiral	The Elements of Effective Communication

Grateful acknowledgment is made to the authors and publishers for permission to reprint the following material:

"Are You a Self-Starter?" (pp. 87-90) by Oscar Schisgall. Reprinted with permission from the July 1966 *Reader's Digest*. Copyright 1966 by The Reader's Digest Assn., Inc. Condensed from Chicago's *American* Magazine.

"Use of Sales Aids and Promotional Material to PRE-SELL" (pp. 69-72), by W. A. MacCalla, Supervisor, Industrial Sales Service, West Penn Power Company.

"Motivating Man to Stay in Sales" (pp. 16-17), by Andrew H. Thomson, as published in *Sales/Marketing Today*, Vol. 14, No. 5, May 1968.

"Professional Selling the Mallinckrodt Way" (pp. 166-192), by W. R. Johnston, Director of Sales for Mallinckrodt, Inc., Hazelwood, Missouri.

© Copyright 1975 by G. Worthington Hipple

All rights reserved. Except for the inclusion of brief quotations in a review, no part of this book may be reproduced or utilized in any form or by any means, electronic or mechanical, including photocopying, recording or by any information storage and retrieval system, without permission in writing from the publisher.

ACROPOLIS BOOKS LTD.
Colortone Building, 2400 17th St., N.W.
Washington, D.C. 20009

Printed in the United States of America by
COLORTONE PRESS Creative Graphics Inc., *Washington, D.C. 20009*

Library of Congress No. 75-13543

ISBN 0-87491-167-2 (cloth)
ISBN 0-87491-168-0 (paper)

*To GWH who,
without any help
made this book possible.*

*GWH is an Aquarius,
but that didn't help;
Chapter 18 of this book did.*

Contents

PREFACE	ix
FOREWORD by Arthur H. "Red" Motley	xi
1. Advice to a (Bored) Young Man or Woman	1
2. Are You Too Busy Chopping Wood to Take Time to Sharpen Your Ax?	3
3. Run for Your Life	7
4. Will You Be Part of the 5 Percent?	11
5. How Smart Do You Have to Be?	19
6. You're a Giant!	25
7. It's Easy to Be a Winner	29
8. The Image-Makers	33
9. Advertising	37
10. Merchandise It and You'll Sell TWO	47
11. Get in on the Big Sell	53
12. You Can't Sell Peanuts at the End of the Parade	61
13. Time Is Silent and Deadly	65
14. Come in, Said the Spider to the Fly	69
15. You Can't Do It Alone	75

16.	Don't Get Too Technical	79
17.	How Much Education Do You Need?	83
18.	Are You a Self-Starter?	87
19.	Retail Selling	95
20.	Distributor Salesmen	101
21.	The Factory Representative	105
22.	Selling Securities	111
23.	Selling Gasoline and Automotive Services	115
24.	Real Estate Sales	121
25.	Selling Insurance	125
26.	Stop Conforming!	127
27.	The Big Sell	131
28.	Sell Yourself Rich	141
29.	Hammer Home the Difference	153
30.	Professional Selling from A to Z	165
31.	Very Useful Vignettes	195
32.	Today Is the First Day of the Rest of Your Life!	203
	Sales Ideas	207
	Index	209

Preface

YOU COULD GO CRAZY TRYING TO READ all the various books written on selling yourself to success. There are over 9,000 books on the subject in the Library of Congress. And every year they get more sophisticated. Today, as a salesman, you're being computerized, and of course there's always "Psycho Cybernetics," which you can't even find in the dictionary.

This progress is understandable. We're in a trillion-dollar economy. There are over two hundred million people in the United States, to say nothing of the burgeoning world market into which we've set sail.

With all this change, let's take a look at something that hasn't changed. You want to buy an item as simple as a shirt, a pair of shoes or a pair of slacks. Your wife wants to buy a blouse, a box of face powder or food at the local market; or your husband needs a new razor or a tie.

This simple shopping is about the same as it was 100 years ago. Ah, but 100 years ago you could be waited on, treated to service, even have your purchase delivered by a courteous delivery man. Now, what do you suppose happened to all those nice ways of yesteryear?

For everyone from the top to the bottom of any company selling its wares to the consuming public I have a message:

Salesmen (and saleswomen) don't need new rules. They need to learn the old ones and apply them!

Sure, we have to keep up with the times and acquire better methods for selling in a changing world, but we can't afford to backslide on the basics. The late Vince Lombardi said:

"I'll beat you with blocking and tackling." He further blueprinted the statement: "All pro teams have men about the same size and speed. The systems are relatively the same. We all get game films of our opposition in action. The edge is in the blocking and tackling." It's true in pro football and it's true in selling. The edge is in the basics.

Anyone can give you selling platitudes until they come out of your ears:

1. "When the going gets tough, the tough get going."
2. "That salesman stays first who puts his customer first."
3. "Salesmen who take no chances have to take what's left over."
4. "Nothing interests Mr. Customer so much as Mr. Customer."
5. "If you make good selling habits, they will make you."

I could give you twenty-five more to add to the ones above. They're from "Sales Memos" put out by Dartnell Corporation. How much they will help you I don't know. What will really help you is a thorough understanding of the basic rules of success.

What you are going to read in this book are the many techniques to SELL YOURSELF RICH—very little theory, all the rest is fact! Anybody can play the game. You all have a chance to make the team. A college education is a plus, but it's not essential. The world is full of successful men who are high school drop-outs. The president of Paramount Pictures, the genius, Mr. Ling, is one. Why, the richest man in the world, Mr. Frederick George, is a grammar school drop-out!

Young or old, you can really be a great, big, money-making salesman. There is only one person standing in your way—YOU!

After you read awhile you'll wonder if I think salesmen do anything right. Well, of course plenty of them do, but plenty of them don't. A coach like George Allen of the Washington Redskins doesn't pay too much attention to his players who are doing the job right. His attention is directed to the ones who aren't doing the job right.

The whole bit reminds me of a story I tell every time I lecture. A rooster is walking through the hen house and sees a large ostrich egg in one of the nests. He calls all the chickens together and says, "Look, I don't want to bawl anybody out, I just want to show you what some of the others are doing."

So start reading. We'll cover it all from gas station salesmen to manufacturer's salesmen and back again. Good luck!

G. Worthington Hipple

Foreword

"SELL YOURSELF RICH has it all. It is backed with the basics of successful selling as developed and practiced by those who have been successful in selling. Read it. It will 'work' for you if you 'work' at it!"

Arthur H. "Red" Motley
*Chairman of the Board
of Parade Publications and formerly
President of the
Chamber of Commerce of the
United States*

"If Napoleon himself, more highly endowed by nature with every military attribute than any other general of the Christian era, thought it essential to teach himself his business by incessant study—how much more is such study necessary for ordinary men?"

Elman Tate

Advice to a (Bored) Young Man or Woman

Chapter 1

DIED, AGE **20**; BURIED, AGE **60**. The sad epitaph of too many Americans. Mummification sets in on too many young people at an age when they should be ripping the world wide open. For example: Many people reading this page are doing so with the aid of bifocals. Inventor? *Benjamin Franklin*, age **79**. The presses that printed this page were powered by electricity. One of its first harnessers? *Benjamin Franklin*, age **40**. Some are reading this on the campus of one of the Ivy League universities. Founder? *Benjamin Franklin*, age **45**. Others, in a library. Who founded the first library in America? *Benjamin Franklin*, age **25**. Some got their copy through the U.S. Mail. Its father? *Benjamin Franklin*, **31**. Now, think of fire. Who started the first fire department, invented the lighting rod, designed a heating stove still in use today? *Benjamin Franklin*, ages **31, 43, 36**. Witty, conversationalist, economist, philosopher, diplomat, favorite of the capitals of Europe. Journalist, printer, publisher, linguist (he spoke and wrote in five languages). Advocate of paratroopers (from balloons) a century before the airplane was invented. All this until the age of **84**. And he had exactly two years of formal schooling. It's a good bet that you already have more sheer knowledge than Franklin ever had when he was your age. Perhaps you think there's no way to think of anything new, that everything's been done. Wrong! The simple, agrarian America of Franklin's day didn't begin to need the answers we need today. GO DO SOMETHING ABOUT IT!

    Tear out this page and read it on your 84th birthday. Ask yourself what took over in your life, indolence or ingenuity?*

*The above was taken from a 100th Responsibility message that appeared in *Newsweek*. *Newsweek* inaugurated this public service series February 13, 1967.

The author lecturing and proving a point.

Are You Too Busy Chopping Wood to Take Time to Sharpen Your Ax?

Chapter 2

1. When did you stop learning?
2. Do you know how sharp you have to be to compete in a trillion-dollar economy?
3. You don't get smarter just because of longevity.
4. What you should do to stay a giant step ahead of your competition.

IF YOU CAN'T LIVE WITH this chapter, if you can't put it to work, bite the bullet or do a swan dive out of a ten-story building. It's simple—you won't make it. You'll exist, but all the dreams you've dreamed will never come true. Being too busy chopping wood is the curse of about 95 percent of all men in most professions. You'll get a dramatic picture of it when you read Chapter Four of this book.

People in the business world are the guiltiest of all of not taking enough time to sharpen their axes.

We only educate the young. There is a cutoff date taken for granted in education. We go to school only as long as it takes us to learn a trade or profession, or the ability to converse in a cultivated fashion, and then we quit—having "become educated" (past tense).

This notion that one has already been educated (past tense) offers one social permission never to read a book again, never to learn anything more, never to have another thought. Is it any surprise that, under such conditions, so many people as they grow older become incapable of moving up in their jobs, whether they be in selling or a service? How do you measure up in your profession?

When I talk to sales rallies, a Chamber of Commerce or a national sales convention, I tell my listeners they could never be carpenters, plumbers or bricklayers. Why? Because they would never swing for all the cash those trades have to lay out for their tools. Hundreds of dollars. Most men have a saw around the house—it's a safe bet you couldn't cut hot butter with it. It's never been sharpened. Next time you get a chance, do yourself a favor. Ask a carpenter to show you his saw and his chisels. You will see that his saw has been almost filed down to a point from continual sharpening. You could almost do brain surgery with his chisels. It is a safe bet that your carpenter does not have a college degree. In most cases he is a high school drop-out, but he is smart enough to know (far better than you) that he can't do good work with dull tools.

Now, once again. How much time have you taken from the TV to sharpen your knowledge? Oh, if you only knew how fast time is running out on you!

You are guilty of being too busy chopping wood if you can't honestly answer "yes" to the following questions:

1. Do you subscribe to the newspaper or magazine about the product you represent? For example, in furniture and appliances there is *Retailing Daily*.

2. Do you subscribe to *Fortune* magazine and read it every month?

3. Do you subscribe to *Business Week* or *U.S. News and World Report* and read it every week?

4. Do you subscribe to *The Wall Street Journal* and read it every day?

5. Have you joined your local Sales and Marketing Executives Club, and do you attend regularly?

6. Have you taken the Dale Carnegie course?

Everything mentioned above is a *tool* in the same sense a chisel is to a carpenter or a trowel to a bricklayer. We white-collar workers are wrong to think we can get away without doing as much sharpening as we do chopping. Salesmen and service people, come alive! You're in a trillion-dollar economy. The Age of Aquarius won't wait for you. It's time to catch up.

I could write pages about what the six suggestions above have done for me. Now I can converse with doctors, lawyers, merchants, chiefs. Can you?

That old opportunity you hear so much about doesn't knock too many times, but it does knock. I know a lot of men who have gone home to their wives, and the dialogue that followed went something like this:

"Well, Henry, did you get the promotion?"

"No, Martha, I didn't. They gave it to Harrison."

"You're kidding. How could they possibly give it to him?"

And then in one word pathetic Henry gives her the answer: "Politics."

And the poor slob believes it. The only trouble with Henry is, he wasn't ready for the company when the company was ready for him. And by now you must know why.

Your suggestions might be all right, but how much is it going to cost me, you may ask.

It will be the cheapest investment you'll ever make. We are now talking about your life! How much money you are going to make. How far you will move up the ladder of success in your vocation. This is for all the chips. The total cost of all the things I suggested you do, from item one to item six, is about $503.50, give or take a buck. Around $42.00 a month. All the items I've mentioned are tax-deductible. They are things that you are doing to keep up with your job. Or, let me put it another way. I've been deducting them for eleven years, have been audited by the IRS three times and they have never said a word about them. All are listed in my business expenses.

I often give a talk using an ax to illustrate my message. I have a log, eight- to ten-inches wide and six feet high, mounted on a four-by-four-foot piece of plywood scored with braces at the bottom. I buy a *brand new* long handled ax for each talk (see the attached picture of me in action). I start chopping away on that log, and do I get that audience's attention! The ones in the front row have to be alert as the chips start flying. Then I stop and for the first time ask them if they're too busy chopping wood to sharpen their ax. Then I walk out into the audience and tell them:

"This is a brand new ax. It is as sharp as sharp can be. Ladies and gentlemen, everytime I take a whack at that log this ax gets duller. It never gets sharper. Think about it. Do you honestly believe because you've been in business X number of years you're getting smarter? We're getting duller in an economy that won't wait. Every day of your life some new system, some better way to do the job is discovered. You won't find out much about it by watching your local TV or reading the sports section of your newspaper."

How well you will do in life will *always* depend on how sharp you are in all departments of your chosen profession. And if you have any doubts, wait until you read Chapter Four, "Will You Be Part of the 5 Percent?"

WHAT YOU CAN DO TO SELL YOURSELF RICH:

The six suggestions outlined above.

Run for Your Life

Chapter 3

1. How you can improve your memory.
2. What you have to do to be a good listener.
3. Why you must be better able to communicate in whatever vocation you choose.

I'VE BEEN LECTURING to sales forces all over the world for over fifteen years. About ten years ago I recorded my first sales record titled, "Sell Yourself Rich," and about three years later I recorded the second, titled, "Hammer Home the Difference," both for the Chicago Businessmen's Record Club. To the best of my knowledge, motivational records all started with the dean, Arthur H. "Red" Motley's record, "Nothing Happens Until Somebody Sells Something." It's a story and a title nobody could argue with. It wasn't so long after Motley and after Jack Lacy's record, "Hot Button Salesmenship," that sales records came on like gang busters; just to mention a few: "How To Sell Better," by Edward J. Hegarty; Charles Roth's "The Moment of Truth—For a Winning Sales Approach"; "Easy Selling," by Charles E. Cullen; followed by records from Earl Nightingale, Zenn Kaufman, Bill Gove, Dr. Arthur Secord, and so on. They were all priced the same. All you had to do was pick the one you thought would make you a world beater. The new look in sales recordings is the switch to cassettes. With them, if you're really dedicated, you can play them in your car while going to work or en route to make a customer call. I'm sorry to say there is a flaw in "forty-five minutes to success" by just listening. How well do you listen? Not so well. How well do you remember? Even worse.

According to Ralph G. Nichols, Chairman of the Communication Department of Minnesota University, it doesn't make any difference whether you hear "Red" Motley, me or anyone else, in person or on a recorded message, unless you are one of the rare people with a photographic memory. Here is what Mr. Nichols has to say about our listening and remembering ability:

"The average person who listens to somebody talk remembers only *half* of what he has heard. And of what he has barely learned, he forgets from *one-half to one-third* within eight hours."

Why all the inattention?

Nichols puts much of the blame on the misuse of spare thinking time. This is how he reasons.

"People think much faster than the 125 words the average American speaks per minute. This leaves spare time to think. You can let your mind wander and miss much of the message or use the following processes designed for more effective comprehension:

"1. Think ahead of the talker, anticipating, if possible where the talk is leading and what conclusions can be drawn from what is being spoken at the moment.

2. Weigh the evidence the talker has used to support the points he makes. Is it valid? Complete?

3. Review and summarize periodically the points of the talk so far completed.

4. Listen between the lines, searching for meanings that might not have been put into words. Watch facial expressions, tones of voice."

Nichols says our brains become over-stimulated—at the expense of good listening—when we hear something that clashes with our most deeply-rooted prejudices, notions, convictions or complexes.

To protect against this threat, he says, hear the speaker out and withhold your judgment until then.

Finally, he calls our inability to listen and remember "a major oversight in our system of instruction."

All I've got to say is that if you can do all the things Mr. Nichols has said, for my money you're one terrific listener.

Here's how I tell it to my audiences:

"Ladies and gentlemen, one of the hardest jobs you will have at this three-day national convention is remembering what you have heard.

"Mr. Ralph Nichols, Chairman of the Communication Department of Minnesota University, says you'll remember about 50 percent of what you hear me say and within eight hours you'll have forgotten one-third to one-half of the new knowledge. In short, you'll get about 16 to 24 percent of what is being said to you." I then repeat this to the audience.

Not so long ago I was talking to three hundred of the top executives in the country at the Greenbrier in White Sulphur Springs, West Virginia. About an hour after I finished my talk one of the men came up to me, slapped me on the shoulder and said, "That was one helluva talk. I'll bet I remember more than 67 percent."

Everytime I tell of that incident the audience laughs—except once. The first time I told it, I only told the audience *once* what Nichols said about how much they would remember. I only said once, "In short, you'll get about 16 to 24 percent of what is being said to you." They didn't laugh the first time because I didn't repeat it twice in a matter of a few minutes. They *had already forgotten* what I said.

IS MAN A FRAUD?

He has all the makings. Every national convention supplies the people attending with pads of paper and pencils to take notes. In all my experience, all my years of watching and giving the audience the best of it, I'd say only about 5 percent take notes. It amuses the heck out of me. I always figured some of them would be smart enough to do it for window-dressing with all the executives around them.

Then to show you how dumb I used to be, I thought maybe they just liked to listen first and then went back to their rooms and made notes. I checked on that. But as soon as the meetings for the day were over it was, "Who's got the cards, the booze, and in what room is the card game going to take place?" Another faction checked on the go-go night spots, and which one had the best topless dancers.

I actually confront them with this when I'm making my talk. It gets a big (if uneasy) laugh. Why? Because as Green, the great cartoonist, said, "They laugh because it's true."

I even say things like:

"Fellows, what if on the last day of the convention the sales manager said, 'Men, something big has come up. Instead of going home, we will all report to this room tomorrow morning at 9 o'clock.'

"And the next morning the sales manager tells all the men to sit down and write about everything that they learned at the convention. 'If you can't do it,' he says, 'you're fired.' And so everyone loses his job." And damned if the salesmen don't laugh again at the truth.

A fable tells of the dog who was asked why he hadn't caught a rabbit. "Well," the dog explained, "I was running for the fun of it. The rabbit was running for his life." What's your incentive? If you really want to be a success in whatever you do, then read this book from cover to cover. You'll forget a lot of it. So read it again and again, and keep putting into practice the lessons you'll learn. Some you already know, and some you don't. Above all else, the time is now! Stop running for the fun of it—start running for your life!

WHAT YOU CAN DO TO SELL YOURSELF RICH:

1. Remember how to be a good listener and why you should be one. Be a note-taker.
2. Learn how faulty your memory really is, and how to remember more by following the rules in this chapter.
3. Remember, if you want to make your point you will have to get your listener's attention—and you may have to repeat your point.

Will You Be Part of the 5 Percent?

Chapter 4

1. The odds are overwhelmingly against success in any profession.
2. Can you afford to live on a pension or social security?
3. How you can shorten the odds against failure.
4. If you've set your mind on making a lot of money—then get into sales.

LET'S GIVE SOME THOUGHT as to why it is so very important for you to think not only of the present but also your future. Many people have researched and proven what I am going to tell you. I'll quote from Earl Nightingale's dramatic way of saying it in one of his many fine recordings:

"If you take 100 men at the age of twenty-five; at the age of sixty-five, of the ones left, one will be very rich. Four will be financially independent. Five will still be working, and fifty-four will be broke or living off of social security or a pension. And this, in the richest country in the world." Mr. Nightingale goes on to point out that only 5 percent will ever make it really big in whatever line of work they choose. You can dream and hope you'll be the rich one, or maybe one of the four financially independent ones. But just dreaming and hoping will surely place you among the fifty-four who will be broke, living off of social security or a pension. If you'll take time to check on your pension or what you are going to get from social security, you'll find you've got a pretty dim future in front of you.

Let's start with one of the best tools to insure against your being one of the fifty-four. It's a tool you don't have to be born with. You can acquire it. It's free, yours just for the taking. It's called *persistence*.

"Nothing in the world can take the place of persistence. Talent will not: nothing is more common than unsuccessful men with talent. Genius will not: unrewarded genius is almost a proverb. Education will not: the world is full of educated derelicts. Persistence and determination alone are omnipotent. The slogan 'Press on' has solved and always will solve the problems of the human race." So said Calvin Coolidge.

I feel sure Coolidge would have cottoned to the late Vince Lombardi, coach of the famous Green Bay Packers football team. He would have appreciated Lombardi's challenge of "Second effort." This is another way of saying persistence and determination are omnipotent.

In case you missed it or have forgotten it, here is what Lombardi had to say about winning:

"Winning is not a sometime thing; it's an all-the-time thing. You don't win once in awhile, you don't do things right once in awhile, you do them right all the time. Winning is a habit. *Unfortunately, so is losing.*"

If you don't think this applies to whatever your job is, here is what Lombardi has to say on that score:

"Running a football team is no different from running any other kind of organization—an army, a political party, a business. The principles are the same. The object is to win—to beat the other guy. Maybe that sounds hard or cruel. I don't think it is. It's a reality of life that men are competitive, and the most competitive games draw the most competitive men. That's why they're there—to compete. They know the rules and the objectives when they get in the game. The objective is to win—fairly, squarely, decently, by rules—but to win."

I've told many an audience I've lectured to that most of us couldn't play football for Vince Lombardi. If we did, he'd soon trade us. If we worked for him in business, he'd fire us. He said, "You've got to pay the price." There are not enough of us who want to pay the price for success. I've often thought one of the cruelest quirks of fate is that all of us are masters of our own destiny. As Armand "Gary" Gariepy puts it, "Your future is in your hands."

Deep down inside an unsuccessful man, despite all his excuses, he didn't want to pay the price. He didn't want to make that second effort. He didn't cultivate the magic of persistence. So he's either one of those still working at sixty-five—or part of the even less fortunate fifty-four, broke or living on social security or a pension.

YOU'RE LUCKY IF YOU'RE IN SALES

In sales you can really make the big money. You're not locked in like most people are. If you want to work late, if you want to work *very* late, you can do it. You can't beat the odds. The man that works harder and longer generally has a better performance record and, with it, bigger take-home checks. Think of all the people you know on a fixed salary. Perhaps they get a raise now and then. It doesn't come close to fighting today's rampant inflation. Today a breadwinner has to be making almost twice what he did just a few years ago just to stay even. And if you doubt that statement listen to these facts. As far back as 1958 a wage earner had to make $6,457 a year to match the purchasing power of a $3,000-a-year income in 1939. And that was long before inflation had started to run wild.

HOW MUCH CAN YOU MAKE SELLING?

This is one time the expression, "The sky's the limit," fits.

Recently I shocked the living daylights out of a bunch of my friends. We were at a dinner party and one of the men gave me a good opening line.

"Where did you make your last talk, Worthington?" he asked.

I told him, with everybody else at the table listening, that I has just returned from talking at a National Convention for National Safety Associates at the Grand Bahama Hotel, West End, Grand Bahama Island.

The friend then said, "Boy, you really have the life. We're up here freezing and you're having fun in the sun."

I laughed and said, "Yes, I did have fun, and it also was a real eye-opener. I talked to about 400 people, all between the ages of twenty-four and thirty years of age. I attended their banquet the last night when they give all the awards to the people who do the best job of selling a fire safety device they distribute."

One of the other men innocently asked, "How much can you make selling stuff like that?"

"The kid that won first prize and a trophy almost as big as he was made $56,000," I said. "He's twenty-eight years old." There was a dull silence for a moment. Some of the people at the table looked at me as if they hadn't heard correctly, or thinking I had my figure wrong. Now I had everybody's undivided attention, so I poured it on. I told them about some others who hadn't come in first, but who made twenty, thirty-five, or forty thousand dollars a year working for National Safety Associates. It's a good thing most of them knew me well enough to know I wouldn't lie to them, because when I told them most of the people selling for National Safety *only sold part time*, that was the cherry on the Charlotte Russe!

I had been sitting next to the vice president of National Safety during the banquet, and after listening to the president tell how much the winner had made and handing him his trophy, I turned to the vice president and asked, "For how many years?"

"Just for last year," he told me. "The boy never saw the inside of a college," he added. Then he told me that he had made $39,000 the first year he sold for National Safety.

There wasn't one man at the dinner party that night when I told them about my talk for National Safety who made anywhere near that kind of money, except myself. I knew that. You might call it a mean streak in me, but I never miss a chance to let people know how much you can make selling. I know without their saying so that they often look down their noses at the selling profession.

But I don't want you to get the idea that what I have just told you about all those young people making scads of money is just one of those quirks, a once-in-a-lifetime happening. It isn't.

A couple of years ago I talked to a group of salesmen at Tantallion Lodge in Missouri, back in the Ozarks. The people at that convention sold kitchenware—pots and pans. I asked the fellow who hired me to talk to his people about how he got into the business. And that was another real lesson in life. Here was his story:

"I used to be a cop. I worked for the vice and bunko squad in the St. Louis Police Department. One night my wife told me that we were going over to a friend's house for dinner. We were going to eat food that was cooked by a salesman for a cookware company. I told her I'd go for the free meal, but we were not going to buy any pots and pans, not on our salary. I was making $350 a month at the time. After we got there I found out that what we were going to eat was sauerkraut. This particular item was picked because of the smell it makes. The salesman could prove there wouldn't be any smell when it was cooked in his cookware. When it was finished and I was asked to try it, I told the man if I ate sauerkraut I'd be up all night with a sick stomach. The salesman insisted I try it, and that if I got sick he'd give me a whole set of the cookware free. That's when I told him I was with the vice and bunko squad, and if this was a racket he was in for it. To make a long story short, I ate the sauerkraut, (and I didn't get sick for the first time in my life). After I considered the salesman who did the selling and his appearance, I had just one thought. Maybe I was in the wrong racket.

"I had already found out how much this guy was making—over twice what I was dragging down as a cop. I quit a month later and have been selling this cookware ever since. Last year I made over forty-four thousand dollars."

Here's a story of my own. I've been associated with The Fedders Corporation, the world's largest manufacturers of room and central air conditioners, for over eighteen years. I started out as a district sales manager when air conditioning in this country was a whole new idea. Salvatore Giordano, the president and chairman of the board, is the only man I ever worked for who always kept his word. He didn't care how much you made working for him as a salesman. It was in my third year that I made over $58,000. In one month I got a commission check for $10,872.22. And don't think I wasn't stunned! I was sure they had made a mistake, despite the fact that we were having a hot summer. The next year they had to raise the salary of the vice president and the comptroller because I, a salesman, had made more than either one of them. And darned if I didn't almost catch them the next year too. The assistant to the comptroller was pretty bitter about what the salesmen were making—he didn't make any bones about it. That check I got for over ten thousand dollars for one month was more than he made for the whole year.

There was no magic about making all that money selling. I was just one of those dummies who found out early in my selling career that if you follow your company's game plan you'll bat about 850. Do it your way and you'll be lucky to bat 500! I'll cover that point in detail later in the book.

Let's talk about selling securities; about being a stock broker, which is a nice name for a salesman. They now call them A.E.'s, account executives, but if they're worth their salt, they have to be good salesmen. Like all salesmen they have their top and bottom. Some stock brokers make over a hundred thousand dollars a year, year in and year out. Some get down to the office at eight in the morning, two hours before the exchange opens. Those same ones stay hours after the market has closed. Some A.E.'s only make about twelve or fifteen thousand a year, coming in later and leaving earlier. They're soon out of the securities business—not because they're not satisfied with what they're making, but because the company isn't satisfied with what they're making. And every one of these people has the same stocks to sell at the same price!

Let's talk about insurance companies. I'm sure you've heard about their million dollar clubs. It is a real mark of distinction for a person to have sold a million dollars worth of life insurance in one year. And again, these men and women all have the same chance to sell more, to make more money. Companies like New York Life, Mutual, and Prudential don't have special training for only some of the salesmen. They don't give special prices to some of them. And they don't have pets that always get the best leads. Again, the winners are the ones who start earlier and work later. As Lombardi says, they don't think selling is a something thing. It's an all-the-time thing. They don't do things right once in awhile, they do them right all of the time.

It doesn't make any difference what sex or color you are, either. Not so long ago I met a black man who was a salesman for an insurance company in North Carolina. In his fifth year with the company he was elected to the million dollar club.

In 1968 Andrew H. Thomson, Vice President of New York Life Insurance Company, had the following to say in a speech delivered to the Sales and Marketing Executives Club of Boise, Idaho:

I recently asked forty of our salesmen with four to forty years' experience to tell what motivated them most in our business. To what things about selling did they respond particularly—what made them tick? Here are the five most important motivators, and why they chose selling, according to these professional salesmen:

1. Freedom of action and independence of operation. As one salesman from the West put it, "I have the right to choose whether I succeed or fail, and I will fail unless I choose to be competitive, efficient and productive."

2. Job security. Security, however has a different meaning to these salesmen. They find their greatest security in a straight commission contract. The sky is the limit—they have no ceiling! They see insecurity only for those saddled with a salary. [Author's note: Let me ask you to read that last line over again.] Their markets, their clientele and their earnings are limited only as their abilities limit them.

3. Satisfaction from helping others. Giving service to their clients was listed, without exception, as one of the greatest of all motivating factors.

4. The challenge of a rough and highly competitive market place. One highly articulate lad from Pennsylvania struck a note that may very well apply to all successful salesmen. "I believe my first motivation to success in this business was the joy of solving problems to which I had the best and sometimes the only solution. If the newer salesman is motivated in this manner, he ceases to be apologetic about his product. Nothing drives a man from our business as quickly as a feeling someone is doing him a favor by buying."

5. A chance for unlimited earnings. Money is important. But these men would not be with us just for money alone. Their greatest motivation comes from job satisfaction. But in giving satisfaction their earnings become unlimited.

John Ruskin said, "No amount of pay ever made a good soldier, a good teacher, a good artist, or a good workman." And he could have added, "A good salesman."

Henry Thoreau said, "Success usually comes to those who are too busy to be looking for it."

We can put to bed the jokes about the salesman and the farmer's daughter. We can forget a crazy cartoon sent to me years ago showing a goofy looking guy with a diploma under his arm. The caption below it said, "Six munce ugo I cutnt evn spel sailesmun and now I are one." Do a good job selling and you can keep right on laughing all the way to the bank.

One last thought before we leave this subject. It was said by the great Jack Lacy, "the hot button salesman."

"Selling is the backbone of the living standard of our country. If it weren't for the salesman, everybody would be working for about half of what they're getting today. Only half the economy is bought—the other half is sold!" Read that last line over and don't ever forget it!

Lacy continues, "The basic secret of the prosperity of anything—an individual, a company, an area, a nation—is how much money circulates through it. The business of the salesman is to get more money into circulation.

"Willpower and memory will enable a man to make calls and repeat what he knows about a product. This will make him a salesman, but only an average one. If he's going to be great, he has to develop a selling imagination."

WHAT YOU CAN DO TO SELL YOURSELF RICH:

1. You can beat the odds against you.
2. The big money is in sales.
3. Follow your company game plan. You'll bat 850 plus. Do it your way, you'll be lucky to bat 500.
4. When you're doing a good job you're:
   a. Insulating job security
   b. Getting the satisfaction that comes with helping others
   c. Beating the challenge of a highly competitive marketplace
   d. Giving yourself a chance for unlimited earnings.
5. And once more, "Only half of the economy is bought—the other half is sold."
6. So go ahead. Beat the odds that say you can't make it! Sell Yourself Rich.

How Smart Do You Have to Be?

Chapter 5

---

1. IQ is not the measure of success.
2. It's attitude not aptitude.
3. Sorry, a college or university degree will not ensure success.

IF YOU WANT TO TALK ABOUT IQ or any other measure of how bright, how intelligent you are, we've got loads of room for argument on the subject.

Do you have to have a college degree or a special kind of talent to make money in selling or in any other field? Let's talk about the IQ factor first. And listen to what my very good friend, the late Armand (Gary) Gariepy, Director of Sales Training International, had to say. He was adamant on the subject. We talked together at many a sales rally, and how I loved to hear Gary burn away at IQ:

"Shame on those who apply the metric system to the human mind and dilute confidence, vitality and the will to do!" was his opening line; and then he'd continue, "We cannot measure the qualities for great performance. Yet these qualifications, inherent in all, may be developed by endless work and self-discipline. You can do anything you set your mind to. Your success is basically contingent on your attitude, not aptitude."

I have no intention of offending the testers, but I think that IQ and aptitude tests have gone too far. They kill ambition, scuttle hopes, weaken desires and block drives as well as undermine the knack of personal development inherent in all of us. For instance a recent report on education by the Rockefeller Brothers Fund warns against blindly following test scores. It says in part:

"Decisions based on test scores must be made with awareness of the imponderables in human behavior. We cannot measure the rare qualities of character that are a necessary ingredient of great performance. We cannot measure aspiration or purpose. We cannot measure courage, vitality or determination."

FOR SUCCESS—STUDY THE FACTS

To what extent would the abolition of testing for innate abilities, capacities for achievement and special aptitudes mentally emancipate your salesmen? Suppose they were alerted to the facts of success? Suppose they knew there was no aristocracy of brains? Suppose they knew that in each of us there are seeds for either extraordinary success or tragic failure? It definitely would make a difference in their efforts and results.

Why not tell them the truth? Why not tell them that the mind is not a container to be filled, but something to be set afire? Make them realize that the brain is like a muscle: the more you use it, the better it works. The more you work it, the more brains you will have to use. Forget all about IQ and aptitude tests. Remember that the high point of human courage is developed and inspired by desperate odds. Can you imagine what these new positive attitudes and self-concepts would do to their sales?

Yet so often we are not taught the fundamentals of success. For example, we often are taught that we are no stronger than our weakest link. That is only a half-truth. We are also as strong as our strongest link. What we really need is an attitude of positive determination. Dilute your fears, gain self-confidence, learn courage which means risk. The enterprising man in every instance risks his money, his face, his time and his talents. He knows he can do anything he sets his mind to. As Will Rogers once put it: "Don't forget, when you're speaking of intelligence, everybody is ignorant, but on different subjects."

ATTITUDE STIMULATES APTITUDE

On this question of attitude vs. aptitude, let's take the case of a boy failing in trigonometry. The principal and the teacher say he hasn't the background or aptitude for mathematics. His father refuses to believe this. He knows that the boy doesn't study and spends all his time with hot rods and dreaming of automobiles. So, to set an example and establish a principle of success, the father offers him the convertible of his choice, provided he at least passes trig. What do you think will be the result? The motivating force will be the result of an aroused attitude, not an aroused aptitude. The aptitude has been there all along.

Gary Cooper, for instance, couldn't make the dramatic club at Grinnell College. He was told he didn't have the aptitude for acting. Wernher Von Braun, who helped put our satellites into orbit, disliked and failed mathematics, but once he became interested in rockets, he quickly became proficient. Sir Winston Churchill attributes his command of the language to the fact that at Harrow his deficiencies in the classics and mathematics kept him in one form for three times the normal length of time.

So that phrase you hear so many times, told to children and adults alike, "You can do anything you put your mind to," is true. You can. And it won't be your IQ or your aptitude that does it, it will be your attitude. Make up your mind you can sell any customer you call on or talk to.

Let me show you another example of the IQ myth being blown apart. It demonstrates once more how powerful your attitude is toward whatever you do.

A fellow by the name of Lou Prato wrote an article called "Football Scouting's Computerized Crystal Ball: Second and Goal." It tells how they used to pick college football players for the pros, by the seat of their pants, with the help of a friendly coach and alumni. Here is the part we're interested in:

THE COMPUTER DECADE

It is the computer, first instituted by Tex Schramm of Dallas in 1962, which more than anything changed the manner and style of pro football scouting. And despite the impersonalization inherent in computerization, those who use it strongly defend the computer's practicalities.

"Using the computer as a group helps cut down expenses," says Blesto's Butler. "I think it would be impossible for one team to afford the personnel and big computer needed to do the job our group does.

"Even I was against the computer when we first started, for I thought it would eliminate people. But I was wrong. It can do in thirty seconds what it used to take a week to do.

"But in all honesty, the computer is only as good as the information you put into it. The machine never picks the football player. We have a saying in this business, 'Garbage in, garbage out.' If your information is bad your result will be, too."

It's this human factor which decomputerizes the relentless objectivity of the machines. The point is that the computers can only minimize the chances of misjudgement. No computer and no scout can accurately measure a player's desire and toughness. [Read that last line again.]

"Last season," Butler says, "there was a classic case of a computer-human error when rookie Don Nottingham of Kent State became a starter and outstanding runner for the Baltimore Colts. Nottingham was the four hundred forty-first and last man drafted in January of 1971."

"Every year, three to fifteen players make the NFL who you didn't give a chance to," said a Cepo Scout.

"The quality you can't measure is what's in a guy," says Jack Butler. "You see a guy on the hoof, and he looks like the greatest, but you're not sure of his temperament. You see another guy that is not quite big enough or fast enough, but he makes the sacrifice; he has the desire. Put it this way: everybody wants to show up on Sunday to play the game, but not all want to sacrifice the other six days."

Let me add just one more example along the Don Nottingham line. Recently at the Washington Redskins training camp a young man by the name of Herb Mul-key showed up to try out. He had never played college football. George Allen, the coach of the Redskins, has so little respect for untested college players that he accidently traded one choice twice! The only thing that keeps Mul-key from playing first string is that he happens to be a back up for Larry Brown. But it doesn't alter the fact that against all odds Mul-key plays for the Washington Redskins. He had that persistence, that determination Calvin Coolidge talked about. It wasn't so much evident aptitude as attitude.

Sure, it's a good idea to have a good education, but don't forget you can also make it without one. If you take education, persistence and determination and put them all together, you've got a triple threat in any ball game.

As far back as forty-five years ago the National Cash Register Company of Dayton, Ohio, had the reputation of being the hottest selling organization in America. This company had a national selling organization which produced and trained such men as Alvin McCauley, who became President of the Packard Motor Car Company; Hugh Chalmers, who became President of the Chalmers Motor Car Company; Thomas J. Watson, President of IBM; Joe Rogers, President and founder of Addressograph Company; Henry Theobold, who founded Toledo Scale Company; A. J. Lawer, who became General Manager of Burroughs Adding Machine Company; and many, many others. This is a record unapproached by any other organization in the history of selling.

How did National Cash Register achieve such a reputation? It was based on ATTITUDE; the attitude of its great founder, John H. Patterson. You must read the book titled, *One Foot in the Door*, by George F. Taueneck. It's the story of Patterson's life. Every specialty salesman and sales executive should read it. The attitude portrayed in the book is the attitude of National Cash Register towards salesmen and towards selling. It became a company creed, and the attitude of those who worked for the company. It was a science of purpose never surpassed and probably never to be approached by any other selling organization.

Attitude—what is it? There is a verse by Ella Wheeler Wilcox which says it rather well:

> Ships sail east, ships sail west
> by the self-same wind that blows.
> It isn't the gale, it's the set of the sail
> that determines the way we go.

Attitude is a state of mind and each of us has the choice of selecting our attitude towards life, people and our job. Don't worry about your IQ, worry about the set of your sail!

WHAT YOU CAN DO TO SELL YOURSELF RICH:

1. Forget aptitude. Concentrate on your attitude.
2. Apply yourself. No machine has been made that can measure your desire or toughness.
3. Your world is full of successful men and women who have confounded the experts. And you guessed it. They did it with ATTITUDE!

You're a Giant!

1. Psychologists say most of us habitually underrate ourselves.
2. You actually have the equipment to be almost anything you put your mind to.
3. You have three ounces of brains. So does the guy next to you and everybody else.

"The most complex machine in the world—your mind—costs nothing to run, no matter how much you use it; and it pays dividends."—Paul DeWitt

THE ONLY TROUBLE IS you didn't know it. That's a fact. Did you know your three ounces of brains can outperform any combination of the best computers so far developed? You can only feed into a computer what has come from somebody's brain.

Until about twenty-five years ago scientists had no idea just how the human brain and nervous system worked to achieve a complicated goal or even something as simple as picking up a shoe. Then man set out to build an electronic brain, to construct goal-striving mechanisms of his own. This science was called cybernetics (from a Greek word which means "Steersman"). Having discovered the necessary operating principles, the scientists asked themselves: Can this be the way the human brain works? Can it be that our Creator provided us with a servo-mechanism more wonderful than any electronic brain ever dreamed of, but operating on the same basic principles? In the opinion of many cybernetics scientists, the answer is yes.

Your subconscious is a mechanism—a goal-striving servo-mechanism consisting of the brain and nervous system, which is used and directed by the mind. This servo-mechanism makes use of stored information or "memory," and it works on data we feed into it (our thoughts, beliefs, interpretations).

So don't forget what Blesto's Butler had to say about information received via computers when recruiting pro football players: "Garbage in, garbage out."

If you feed the information into your mind that you are inferior, undeserving or incapable (a negative self-image), that's just what you'll get. Do just the opposite and your internal mechanism will work automatically to achieve goals of success. Now keep in mind that psychologists say *most of us habitually underrate ourselves*—so it behooves us to correct it.

This isn't as difficult as it may first appear. Your automatic mechanism can't tell the difference between an actual experience and one that you imagined. The information available to it is what you *believe* to be true. That, and that alone, is the information it acts on. So again, if we continually picture failure to ourselves, our impersonal mechanism will reward us with failure-type responses and emotions. The reverse is true when we picture ourselves as successful and confident.

Walk up to your first prospect of the day thinking, "I'll never sell this guy," and you stand a good chance of being right. Reverse the thought and make the sale.

The famous psychiatrist, Dr. Alfred Adler, got off to a bad start in arithmetic when he was a schoolboy. His teacher became convinced that he was "dumb in mathematics." Adler passively accepted the evaluation, and his grades seemed to prove it. One day, however, he had a sudden flash of insight and announced that he thought he could solve a problem the teacher had put on the board which none of the other pupils could work. The whole class laughed, whereupon Adler became indignant, strode to the blackboard and worked the problem.

Nick Buoniconti, the star linebacker for the Miami Dolphins pro football team, is considered small for the job. It is said he makes up for it in speed and determination. While he was sitting in the Boston office of a law firm, one of the law partners asked Buoniconti what he was going to do after his football playing days were over. Buoniconti said he would like to become an attorney. The other man smiled, gave a little shake of his head and said, "Football players don't make good lawyers." That did it, so far as

Buoniconti was concerned. He enrolled the next week in law school. Today he is a good practicing attorney, when he isn't giving his competition a fit on the football field.

In this chapter I am trying to make one point very strongly. You have the equipment to be almost anything you put your mind to. I want to take away any chance of your using such an alibi as, "I'm just not smart enough. I don't have the brains Walter has." You've got the same three ounces he has. If he's selling better it's because he's using his God-given equipment and you aren't. Think about it.

WHAT YOU CAN DO TO SELL YOURSELF RICH:

1. You own one of the most complex machines in the world, your mind. Do you use part of it, or all of it?
2. It may sound corny, but it's true. What you put in is what you'll take out.
3. If you <u>don't think</u> you can sell your quota, make a good advertising presentation, sell a contract or make a good talk, I'll bet you'll be right. And I'll double the bet you've got the makings of a failure. What your subconscious mind <u>believes</u> is what it will act on.
4. Whatever a man thinks he can do is already an accomplished fact—so believe in yourself!

It's Easy to Be a Winner

Chapter 7

1. Because your competition is lousy, it's easier for you to win.
2. You're always just a whisker away from moving up.
3. The difference between win, place and show is yours for just the taking.

IT MIGHT SOUND CYNICAL, even cruel, but you've got to face up to the fact that you're wallowing in a world of mediocrity. It hurts even more when you realize that if you fail you've done it against lousy competition. Every sporting event would like to have a schedule like yours.

Fact: 20 percent of the salesmen sell 80 percent of the merchandise sold. Fact: Only 5 percent will really make it big. That means the odds are 20 to 1 against you. Ah, but it's that 95 percent that's your main competition. You should be able to rise above them with a little extra effort.

The late Armand "Gary" Gariepy had an interesting way for salesmen to judge themselves. He called it the cruel evaluation of the average man. He'd show you a diagram from one to twenty. Number one represented the best. In the middle was number ten labeled average. At the bottom was the label, lousiest.* There was an asterisk next to it with the following explanation at the bottom of the chart: *We are not proud of this word, but there is nothing more semantically correct for this purpose.

Gariepy goes on to say, "Individuals alerted to this diagram will no longer find 'peace of mind' when classified as AVERAGE, which in actuality means the BEST of the LOUSIEST, and the LOUSIEST of the BEST!"

With the new concept provided by this diagram, anyone can see that no one can stand still on the scale of success. We either get better or worse. The movement is by imperceptible degrees. Successful people *consciously* plan to become better and better, bit by bit, day by day; but those who fail, *subconsciously* and unknowingly, become less and less adequate, bit by bit, day by day. No one ever succeeds all of a sudden, or fails all at once! And, as a twentieth century sage remarked: "Yes, pick your rut carefully, as you are going to be in it the rest of your life."

And another wise sage said, "If you're not a better salesman today than you were yesterday, you'll be still worse tomorrow."

I was talking at a sales rally with Earl Nightingale when I first heard him expound on the theory that only 5 percent of us will ever make it big. I was sitting in the first row. I turned around and looked at that vast audience of over 1,800 salesmen and thought to myself—only a little over ninety in this audience have a chance. The rest of them might as well quit. It's like telling you I'm going to set you back twenty yards in a hundred-yard dash for openers.

But remember, I never want you to stop chasing that 5 percent. While you're doing it, I want you to tower over the 95 percent around you.

Keep in mind that the great Ted Williams, one of the greatest hitters of all time, never batted 1000, 750 or 500. His best year was a 400 year. Of course, the difference between a 400 hitter and a 300 hitter is a lot of dollars in the pocket. By the same token there's a big chunk of difference between a 250 or 275 hitter and a 300 hitter. Consider the few points you have to move up to be a little something extra, to make that extra money every week. Here is a good example. It happened to me.

I was a salesman with twenty-one other men working for Schenley Distillery out of their Chicago office. We were engaged in a big sales drive. Besides the chance of winning some good prizes, our jobs were on the line, as they always are.

The job was actually making what they called placements in the liquor industry. If the salesmen got enough placements of this new brand, then Schenley would come in with a million-dollar advertising program. The reasoning is simple: Don't advertise until the new brand is on the back bar of the taverns and the shelves of the liquor stores.

To be honest I didn't think I was doing too well. To show you how right I was, I was sixteenth in the standings after the first week. True, I had a nice alibi to hide behind; I was the newest and youngest of all the salesmen. I went to see my father. He could sell you a peanut butter sandwich in the Gobi Desert. After I explained how hard I had been working and my miserable results to date, he thought about it for a few minutes, and then asked me if I'd do him a favor. If I did what he was going to tell me, I'd make more placements. Of course I told him I would and waited for him to give me the magic formula.

"Worthington," he started, "right now you're like most salesmen. Here's what I want you to do." And looking down at me over his glasses, he said, "It won't be as easy as it sounds. I want you to make one, just one, more call each day. You think you can do that?"

"You mean that's all?" I answered.

"That's all." He nodded.

It wasn't the answer I was looking for but I was ready to try anything. I followed the advice, faithfully. The first day nothing happened. It was the same on the second day. On the third day I got my first *extra* placement. Nothing happened on the fourth day, but on the fifth I got TWO extra placements. By the end of that campaign I had moved up from sixteenth to fourth place. The results kind of reminded me of Gariepy's line, "Take it by the inch, it's a cinch; take it by the yard, it's hard."

Just that little extra effort took me out of the "lousy" class, out of being average.

When I was that young whiskey salesman I used to wonder about men who were captains of industry. I'd hear statements made by them or ideas put forth by them, and like you, I thought they didn't sound too smart. Well, I got the answer to that from the same man who told me how to get more placements, my father. I had been telling him about some of the dumb moves I thought the president of the company was making, and that I didn't think he was so smart.

"Oh," my father said, "he isn't so smart, but he's just that much smarter than you." And he held his thumb and index finger so close together you could hardly slip a piece of paper between them.

"Worthington," he continued, "don't ever forget you only have to win the Kentucky derby by a whisker, a photo finish. First place wins over a hundred thousand dollars. Second place drops to fifteen or twenty thousand."

Years later I used the same idea on my audiences. I'd tell them a small margin can make you a big winner. Palmer and Snead don't have to win the masters by five strokes or even a stroke and a half. Juse one stroke will do it. The difference between winning and losing goes from twenty, thirty or forty thousand dollars down to seventy-five hundred or ten thousand for second place. But the next time you see the results of one of those big golf tournaments in the newspaper please study it very closely. Note the difference is just one lousy stroke in the money that can be won *all the way down the line.*

O.K.? O.K., there's all kinds of room for you to move up and make more money against the competition you face every day. It just takes that little added effort.

A LATE FLASH:

I'm watching the final eighteen holes of the afternoon televised Glen Campbell Los Angeles Open Golf Tournament. Jack Nicklaus is getting ready to putt on the eighteenth hole when the announcer says, "If Nicklaus misses this putt, he'll finish in sixth place; if he makes it, he'll tie for second." One stroke was the difference. (So you won't always wonder, Jack missed the putt and ended up in sixth place. You can't win 'em all.)

WHAT YOU CAN DO TO SELL YOURSELF RICH:

1. You can <u>move up in class</u> because 95 percent of your competition is weak. The importance of the above statement is that you'll hate yourself every morning if you fail against the competition around you.
2. Go the Vince Lombardi route. Every day from now on promise yourself to give that little added effort which can move you from twentieth to ninth place or from ninth to win, place or show.

The Image-Makers

Chapter 8

1. How most companies lose millions of dollars worth of business each year—and never get it back.
2. Any man or woman who represents any company is an image-maker.

TRY, IF YOU CAN, TO IMAGINE the president of General Motors issuing an order for the men on the line to leave a few of the bolts or nuts off each car. Try to imagine the president of one of the airlines telling a stewardess to forget to serve you on a dinner flight; to bring you a glass of wine when you asked for a bourbon on the rocks; to snap at you when you asked when the flight would get into New York. Try to imagine the owner of a service station giving the people working for him the following orders: Don't clean the customer's windshield; don't check the oil in his car. If that same customer needs air in one of the car's tires tell the customer, "The air is over there," and point to it.

Not in your lifetime will any of the above things happen at the request of the two presidents or the service station operator. They won't happen at the request of the sales manager, the supervisor or the foreman. They will happen because of the image-makers, who outnumber management by one hundred thousand to one. These people can be the great destroyers. They can cause more havoc in a minute than the seven-year locust.

Every man and woman in selling or service is an image-maker for the company he represents. The trouble is that most of them don't represent the company very well.

So many times I've heard some fellow say to me, "I wouldn't fly such and such an airline." And I always say, "Why, do you know the president?" And his answer is always similar: "No, I wish you could have heard the answers I got from that girl who sold me the ticket." Or, "I had to wait for almost thirty minutes to get my luggage."

Image-makers are the name of the game. They are absolutely the most important people in the selling and service world we live in.

Once I asked my wife why she still went to the bank she was using. We had moved, and she passed another bank now on her way home. Her answer was, "I like the teller." Isn't that a great reason for depositing over two hundred and fifty thousand dollars a year from her business? That teller was a good company representative.

I asked a very good lady friend of mine why she shopped at a small local market, Magruders, instead of at the A&P, the Safeway, or the Giant Food chain. Her answer was, "I like the checker." Just as my wife didn't know the head of her bank, my friend didn't know the president of Magruders or even the manager.

My wife has tons of merchandise delivered to her store during the year. She tells me that almost all of the men will bring the heavy cartons into the storage area except one. He tells her he is "union" and that's as far as he goes, to the door, period. That one man creates the image for the union and the trucking company he works for. She solved her problem in a very simple way. She just told all the companies she buys from she will not accept any merchandise shipped via that particular trucking company.

One of the hardest things to get across to the average worker is the direct effect he has on the company he works for. The last time I had the oil changed in my car the young man who did the job left the oil cap off. By pure luck, I looked under the hood about three hours later. Oil had sprayed all over the motor. If I hadn't looked, one fine day I would have wondered why my motor was completely shot. I went back to the service station. The young man, not very concerned, said, "Yeah, I saw it as soon as you left. Sorry about that." And I, like most people, will take it out on the owner and the product he represents. But you and I know it was really the fault of a poor image-maker at work. These people never stop eroding their company's image. Day in and day out, they shatter millions of dollars' worth of national advertising with their poor responses to customers who have been motivated by advertising to come in and have a look.

Now, in all fairness to the image-maker, we have to place a great part of the blame on his company, his boss or his supervisor. The experts say the child is a product of his home. This also applies very strongly to the worker. He is a product of the company he represents, and the company he represents does not do a good enough job of training and retraining.

I would suggest to management that they take the same approach that all coaches do in the pro sports. Keep in mind that the pro football players and basketball players are stars before they ever arrive in the pro ranks, and yet they constantly get new training and retraining day in and day out during the season. I suggest it isn't enough in today's world for management to feel they can do the whole job with a once-a-year sales meeting.

Work hard at being a good image-maker and someday you may become an executive, or even president of the company you work for. I know a lot who have!

WHAT YOU CAN DO TO SELL YOURSELF RICH:

1. Do you really like the image you create in the minds of all the people you service? Think about it from the customer's viewpoint.
2. If you are not creating a good image, and comfort yourself with the idea that it is OK because the company holds the bag, you're in really big trouble.
3. Companies keep rolling along. Bad image-makers roll themselves right out of a job.
4. If you are not doing a good job for the company you represent, changing jobs won't help. You'll just be a bad image-maker in another company or another field.
5. One wonderful thing about good image-makers is that they have a priceless advantage—job security! The boss can depend on them to keep customers coming back.
6. Put your best foot forward, on the job and off—always! You'll be creating a good image not only for your company but also for yourself.

Advertising

Chapter 9

---

1. Advertising is the best one-two punch in moving people.
2. There are many facets to total advertising.
3. Many people have to work together to make an advertising campaign successful, from politics to selling.
4. How much did you spend last year advertising <u>yourself?</u>

LET'S TALK ABOUT MY PET SUBJECT, advertising, in depth. It is, without a doubt, the greatest weapon you have in selling. You've got the football, and how well you do will depend a great deal on the blocking in front of you. Think of advertising in that light. Later we'll touch a little on people's adverse reaction to anything new. I've made the statement that "familiarity disarms opposition." Think about it. There have been times when you met someone whom you didn't like right off the bat. And haven't you had to say, like most of us eventually do, "You know, now that I've gotten to know Walter, I like him a lot." Familiarity disarms opposition.

Too many people in sales have a tendency to take advertising for granted. "So we've got advertising, big deal." It is just that, a big deal! If you really want to beat your brains out, try selling an unknown, unadvertised product. I know it's murder. I used to be a whiskey drummer for Schenley Distillers right after the repeal of Prohibition. One day they decided to open up a new division. It would be known as The Joseph F. Finch Division. And I was going to get a real break—I was going to be the state manager for this new division in the state of Wisconsin. The first three or four times I told a distributor or dealer I was with the Joseph Finch Division they looked at me as though I was from another world. The next time I walked in, this was my opening line: "I'm Mr. Hipple, with Schenley Distillers, the Joseph Finch Division." That did it. I was riding on the well-known name of Schenley, at that time number one, and one of the biggest advertisers in the country.

I've actually had people, who, on the face of it, looked normal, say to me, "Advertising doesn't work for me." I made one man an offer. I told him if that was true the two of us could make a million dollars. I'd put him in a glass case and take him all around the world like Tom Thumb. People could look at the only guy in the world that advertising didn't work for. We'd charge fifty cents a look. (The bum backed out.)

Now let's go from the ridiculous to the sublime. We must establish in your mind once and for all that, if you're in selling or service, advertising is one of your giant weapons. It doesn't make any difference how big or how small your business is.

In 1954 my wife and I and our two daughters moved to Hunter Mill Farm in Oakton, Virginia. One of the things we inherited when we got there was one of the greatest strawberry patches I've ever seen. We had so many we didn't know what to do with them. One day my teenage daughters decided to put some of them in boxes and sell them for fifty-cents a box. They went down to the front gate and set up shop. When I arrived home they had been there for about two hours and hadn't sold one box of their strawberries. I didn't say anything to them. I drove up to the house, got a big piece of board and painted "Fresh Strawberries, 50¢ a box!" on it and went back to the girls. A half an hour after that sign was nailed to the fence next to their wares, they were back in the house. They had sold all their strawberries. They had a good product; the price was right; but they had forgotten that priceless ingredient, advertising. The giants don't.

Suppose you were head of a mammoth company and I came to your office and said, "Mr. President, I've just found a way for your company to save $203,000,000." Inasmuch as your gross sales didn't even reach that figure, you'd begin to think I was a little nuts. Now get this: If Proctor and Gamble were sure you would remember that Ivory Soap is 99.44% pure and that it floats, that "Tide's in and dirt's out," then they wouldn't have had to advertise in 1970. However, they spent that $203,000,000 to make sure you do remember those products. Why, because they love the advertising agencies? No, they advertise because it *works*. Don't lose any sleep over Proctor and Gamble spending that much money advertising. They did over two billion dollars' worth of business in 1970. Their advertising must have paid off.

Now that we've established that it works, from the biggest to the smallest, let's have a look at how advertising is used.

ADVERTISING AGENCIES

I'll never understand them. When you put on a multi-million-dollar advertising campaign for a company, they sure as hell want it to be successful. If it isn't, next year they will have lost a very lucrative account. If you don't know, even with hundreds of thousand of dollars spent on TV and radio, you must tie it in with local point of sale advertising. This part is left to the company and their salesmen. And that, my friend, is where the advertising agencies die. The company's salesmen let them down. If they were smart, the agency would have one man on the account besides the account executive who did nothing but see that there was a complete follow-through on point of sale advertising material. I'd hate to tell you how many agencies I've seen lose an account for just the reason I've mentioned.

Here's an example of what I mean. A man is sitting home reading the newspaper. He reads an ad about Ancient Age whiskey. He likes what he's read and decides to buy that brand. The next day he comes home with a bottle of Seagrams 7 or Early Times. What happened? What negated that ad he read? When he gets to the liquor store he sees a beautiful window display on Seagrams 7 or Early Times. When he gets inside the store he sees a mass display of those brands, point of sale cards, etc. And without even realizing it, he walks out with anything but Ancient Age. When this happens enough times the company gets the idea their advertising isn't working. It's working, but at half steam. Even the owner of the store finds himself pushing the brands that have been put in the window display and point of sale material. I know, I used to do it, and it always worked for me and the others who did the same. The only trouble is, enough salesmen don't make that extra effort. They have the assorted alibis. The dealer wouldn't let them put up the signs, he didn't want a window display. Hogwash!

The same thing is true for the appliance business. I was in it for eighteen years. The man who does the most with the advertising rises to the top. You put something in, you get something back.

I was a sales manager for an appliance distributor. We had the Motorola, Fedders, and Bendix washer lines. Motorola carried their end of the load with national and local advertising of all kinds. They sold us, on a co-op basis, spec sheets, window displays, wall banners, etc. I visited one of our better dealers in early December. He didn't happen to know that I specialized in window displays. I asked him if I could put in a nice Christmas window display for him.

"You!" he exclaimed.

"Yes, me, Jerry, and it'll be the best one you ever had. I'll bring the display material—you set the date." I won't go into all the details of a good window display, but when I was all through we went outside and looked the window over. He was happier than a pig in mud. After we went back inside he realized we had put all but about three of his radios in the window display. I said, "We can take some of them out, Jerry. "He looked at me as if I was going to throw a rock through his window and said, "I'll tell you what you do. Send me six more of the maroon, four of the green and six of the gray." So by doing something for my customer—tying in with the national advertising and getting his window loaded with Motorola products against all my competitors—I walked out with a nice order without even asking for it. Advertise it and you'll sell *one*, merchandise it and you'll sell *TWO*. That's what I did.

I had a fellow that used to work for me out of Schenley's Chicago office. His one sterling quality was that he followed orders and instructions. When I hired Max I told him the key to making plenty of sales in his territory was getting window displays with our different brands in the taverns and liquor stores and to put up as much point of sale advertising as he could. When Max left the loading dock on Monday mornings he had so much point of sale advertising material in his car he couldn't sit up straight to drive the car. About six months after Max had been on the job the advertising manager for Schenley came to Chicago. He told Lou Golan, head of the midwestern division the following:

"Lou, you tell me who has this particular territory and I'll tell you who's your top salesman." Golan laughed because he knew it was the first time the man had been in Chicago for Schenley.

The advertising manager said, "I just spent fifty-four bucks in a cab driving from one end of the city to the other." To make a long story short, when they checked, the advertising manager was right. It was Max's territory. If you wondered about some of the other salesmen, they didn't want to get their hands dirty. They didn't want display material that was too big. They liked key chains and small displays that wouldn't clutter up their cars. And they were failures.

Advertising has many facets. For example, a good salesman should know something about newspaper advertising. He should first understand the importance of continuity. He should be able to show and convince a dealer of the futility of a single ad. In most cases it's money wasted, and the dealer will remind the salesman that the one ad he ran didn't pull.

The good salesman will carry a copy of every ad that his company runs locally or nationally. He should have a copy of every TV or radio ad his company runs. And be sure he shows it to every one of his dealers. There is a crazy assumption by far too many salesmen and people in general that if you run an ad, everybody has seen it. No, no, no.

Let me tell you about an ad I cut out of a magazine that makes my point. The ad shows a man sitting at his desk. The lead line in the ad says this: "I'm sorry, but I missed your big television spectacular!" Then it goes on, "I manage a supermarket. I spend an average of sixty hours a week on my job. I have little time to watch television. Perhaps you did spend thousands of dollars on time and talent to tell my customers about your product. But you didn't tell me what I could do to make that advertising pay off in my store. But I do know that properly timed merchandising action at the store level can make advertising doubly effective." And that says it all!

Here's a prime example of how you can blow a good advertising campaign. And it isn't fiction or theory. It happened to me in a downtown Washington, D. C., department store.

I was looking for some Christmas presents "for the man who has everything." I saw an ad in the *New Yorker* magazine—full-page, four-color. It was advertising giant bath towels. They called them V.I.P. bath towels. They had a duck on one for the hunter; they had crossed golf clubs for the golfer, and "V.I.P." printed on the third one. On all of them you could include the initials of the man you wanted to give them to. I made the long trek downtown to buy four of them at $12.50 each. I found the right department, told the young lady behind the counter what I wanted, and placed the ad from the *New Yorker* in front of her. She gave it a quick look and her head started wagging as she said,

"We don't have any."

"But it says so right her in the ad, Miss. Are you sure you don't have any?"

Clipping each word as it came out, she said, "I told you, we don't have any." I was just about ready to walk away nursing a slow burn when I looked up, and there on a bar in back of the sales clerk hung the V.I.P. towels. I had to wait a moment to get hold of myself. My first impulse was to grab this young lady by the hair, spin her around and yell, "What the hell are those!"

Instead, I said quietly, "Could I buy the ones hanging above your head in back of you?" Slowly she turned, looked at them and then back at me. No apologies; no "I'm sorry, I didn't know we had them"; just, "Yes."

Now, how would you like to be the president or sales manager of the company that makes those V.I.P. bath towels? How would you have liked to have laid out the money it cost to run a full-page, four-color ad in the *New Yorker* magazine and come within a whisker of failing? Failing because somebody didn't do his job. How many people? The store buyer, the local sales representative and, most of all, the image-maker: the young woman who waited on me.

This sort of thing is happening every minute of every day. I used to have a boss who would make us do the following every time Schenley ran an ad on one of their brands, and God help you if he ever found out you didn't use the following opening line:

"Hello, Harry, I saw your ad in *Life* magazine today."

"My ad; what the hell are you talking about?" I used to hear. Then we had to whip out *Life* and place it in front of him.

"This full page ad on I. W. Harper." He'd look at it and before he could say anything I'd say, "You sell Harper, don't you?" He'd wag his head. Maybe he thought I was nuts, but one thing was for sure: he knew we ran that I. W. Harper ad.

I don't care how much money your company spends on advertising, from newspapers and magazines to radio and TV. Don't ever forget that story about the man who said, "I'm sorry I missed your big television spectacular." In too many ways, millions of people miss your advertising every day.

What do you suppose 95 percent of all salesmen would say if I asked them the question, "How much money of yours did you spend advertising yourself this year?" Well, let's not use that kind of language. Let's just talk about some of the advertising you can do that will put you head and shoulders above your competition. For openers take a look at the picture below:

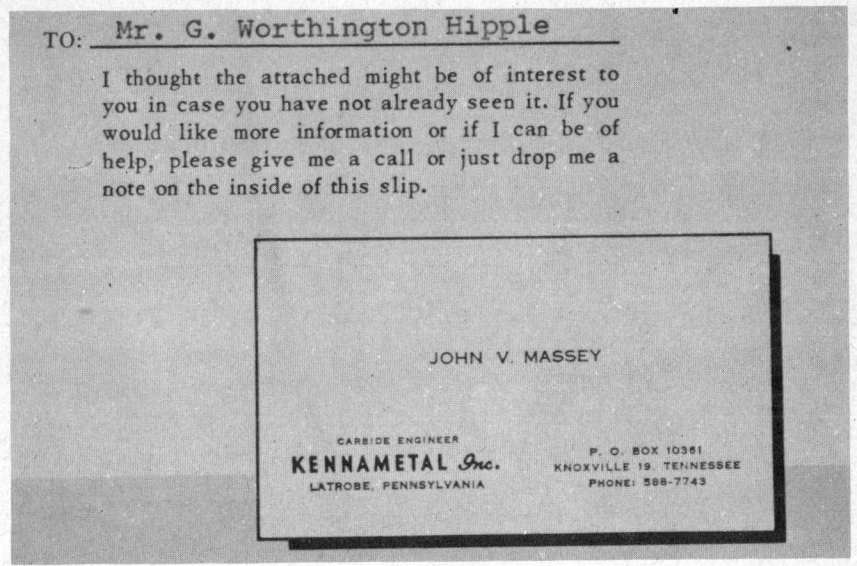

An inexpensive, but rewarding way to establish your credibility even when you're not there

O.K., now that you've read it, let's talk about how powerful a sales aid it can be. First it costs peanuts to produce. Hand the local printer your card and tell him to make up 500 for you.

1. You use it to send your customers that ad your company is running on your new electric shaver, power saw, or health insurance plan. (Maybe you'd better have 1000 printed up like I did.)

2. And this is dynamite! You see in a newspaper, magazine or on TV something about a customer of yours. It might be a picture

of him being elected president of the local Elks, it might be a picture of his wife winning a local golf contest, or it might be a picture of someone else in his family. You might have heard him on TV as I recently heard a customer of mine. You attach your card and mail him the picture or article. Does he want an extra copy? Yes, he wants all the pictures he can get of himself. All the articles he can get that have mentioned him. But he's like you and me—he'd like to make a stab at being modest, or he'd have run out and bought a hundred copies. He'll like and appreciate the one you sent.

This is another true story. A friend of mine was calling on an account up in Boston. He said he made call after call and never even got more than a hello. One day he saw a picture in a Boston newspaper showing a certain kid making the winning hockey goal at a local college. It was such an unusual name that the salesman thought it might be the big buyer's son. He sent the picture with the folder we're talking about. The next time he called on the store, he swears by all that is holy, the man spotted him, walked over and shook hands with him and before he left the store he had his first order. Corny, maybe, but little things mean a lot. Anytime you take the time to show someone else you're just a little more interested than the other fellow, you'll make progress in any line of endeavor.

Now don't be dumb enough to tell your company about this idea, and tell them they should make these folders up for you. They just might do it. Then all the rest of the salesmen will have them too—and all's fair in love and selling.

I know a guy who carries a pocketful of the best hard candy you ever tasted with him at all times. Darned if he doesn't put a piece in your hand every time he meets you. He's not only a helluva salesman, but he always has people mentioning his name. And they always follow it by saying, "He's with the Mayer Company; they make luggage."

Did I get a lesson in spending some of my own money to make money! I had these records of mine to sell and had a kind of corny folder I used to hand out when I talked at a convention or sales rally. One day, Alvin Epstein, one of my very best friends who is in advertising, said to me, "Worth, you know what you should do?" He didn't give me time to answer, but continued, "You should get some billboard matches. The three-inch size. On one side you print 'Sell Yourself Rich' with a picture of you; on the back side you print 'Hammer Home the Difference'; and on the inside you have a regular little order form. Put 'em out at every table where you talk. People kind of freeze up when they see a folder about buying something, but they'll all pick up a book of matches and shove it in their pockets."

I did it. I had Alvin do the design and artwork for me. The only thing he didn't tell me was that you had to buy 30,000 books for an opening order.

Today I can absolutely tell you how many records I will sell, give or take ten, by the amount of matches I give away. Not only that, but I'm now selling two records at a time instead of one. Alvin was right—they put 'em in their pockets. I might get some orders a couple of days after I've talked, but I've gotten some a month, yes, as long as three months later. The more you tell 'em—the more you sell 'em!

Of course, you don't *have* to do any of these things we've been talking about. You can go on in the same old rut, but while you're doing it, keep repeating the following, "Unusual action creates unusual results."

Sometimes you might start to backslide a little. When you feel it happening, re-read the chapter on advertising.

One day my father said to me, "Worthington, did you know that William Wrigley, Jr., the gum king, used to have a partner?"

I said, "No, I didn't."

"Yes, it wasn't long after he and his partner went into business that Wrigley had what was at the time one big electric sign put up on Broadway in New York City. The partner told Wrigley he was nuts, or words to that effect. He said any man who would spend that kind of money advertising a penny stick of gum would soon be out of business. That's when the partnership ended."

In discussing advertising it must be understood that it's hard to measure because it's an intangible. You can yell, "Let your fingers do the walking through the Yellow Pages," all you want, but it's not as though you can say, "I spent this much money and I have five boxes full of something to show for it." You've just got to be a believer—not on faith, but on the facts. I told you this in the beginning. The only reason Proctor and Gamble spend over two hundred million a year on advertising is because it *works*!

WHAT YOU CAN DO TO SELL YOURSELF RICH:

1. First, "You gotta believe!"
2. Be sure and pick out a good way to advertise yourself. Remember? I use the matches to keep my name in front of the consuming public.
3. By all means use the inexpensive folders shown in this chapter to keep your name (and your company's) in your customer's mind when you're not there. It costs so little and is so effective.
4. Be sure and show every ad your company runs in the newspapers and magazines. And ask your customer if he heard and saw your commercial on radio or TV. Don't ever get the crazy idea your customer sees all the ads your company runs. He doesn't.
5. Every successful salesman I've ever known or heard about uses ALL the company's point of sale material. Don't pick and choose, use it all!

Merchandise It and You'll Sell TWO

Chapter 10

---

1. How the author has used merchandising to sell more.
2. Other examples of how people in all types of selling have out-merchandised their competition.

IN OUR LAST CHAPTER WE TALKED about the power of advertising. What an excellent tool it is for breaking down the built-in block most people have towards a new product and to keep reminding them of an old one.

You won't learn much about the word merchandising by looking in the dictionary. I tried three of them plus Roget's *Thesaurus*. I came up empty so far as we know it and apply it to selling.

How the picture has changed in marketing! I'll never forget the time I was to speak at a sales meeting for McKesson Robbins, the big pharmaceutical house. I kept looking at my watch and finally asked the sales manager why we didn't start.

"The merchandising manager isn't here yet," he said in a voice that indicated the Great White Father hadn't arrived. I found out later the merchandising manager was really the top dog. The king pin in department stores today, right under the president and general manager, is the merchandising manager.

So let's not worry about the definitions, then, but go into some good examples of just what merchandising is and how it works.

Take a good look at the picture on page 49. It was made a long, long time ago of myself with my boss. He was the sales

47

manager of Schenley's Chicago office, and I was his assistant. Schenley had just brought out a new brand of whiskey called "Black Label." It was a blend of 65 percent neutral spirits and 35 percent aged whiskies, five, six and seven years old. This was a step ahead of our competition at the time, and I was thinking of a way we could dramatically get into all the retail stores and taverns. I wanted some kind of a grabber, an opener for my salesmen other than the old, "Hello, Charlie, nice weather; I see the Cubs won another one."

I called up a company that manufactured dice, the same ones you use to shoot craps. I asked him if he could make me up a set of three dice: one with five's on all sides, one with six's on all sides and one with seven's on all sides. There was dead silence. I thought he'd hung up on me. I quickly explained what I wanted to use them for and that I would need thousands of them if the company liked the idea. He said he could make them and assured me he could deliver. Three days later I had the three sample dice and went into my boss' office.

"Jake," I said, "I think I've got a good merchandising idea to help our salesmen and to back up our national advertising."

"Vot is it, Vorthington?" (He could never pronounce "W's.")

I pulled the dice out of my pocket and tossed them in front of him on his desk top.

"Vot the hell is this?"

"Five, six and seven-year-old whiskey in the all-new Schenley Black Label."

He had the dice in his hand looking at them. He had done what I wanted him to do. He had done what I thought any dealer would do if a salesman tossed the dice on a dealer's counter. Jake dropped the five and six on the counter with the remark, "A man could roll eleven every time with these." I kept talking about what we could do with the idea, but it was no sale.

I took my idea to another fellow in our "Three Feathers" Division. I told him Jake wouldn't go for it, so they might as well use it with their counter Schenley brand, "Three Feathers," which would also have five, six and seven-year-old whiskey in its blend.

I was in Jake's office when the national sales manager came in from New York. While the three of us talked, a large box was delivered to Jake's office. It didn't indicate what was in it, so Jake

This dice idea, created by Mr. G. W. Hipple, who is standing on the right with the Whiskey Bottle, was used to promote one of Schenley Distiller's biggest national campaigns to put over the idea of five, six and seven-year old Whiskeys and Blends.

Fifty thousand sets of these were made up and used by all salesmen throughout the country. In essence, the idea was that the salesman walked in and threw the three dice out on the counter. Regardless of how he threw them, they came up five, six and seven. When the dealer asked, "What's that?"—the salesman went to work on him, starting with five, six and seven-year old Whiskey and Schenley Reserve.

told me to open it. There in neat rows were five thousand little white boxes, each holding three dice.

The sales manager said, "Oh, yes, here's a good idea we got from Greenfield of the 'Three Feathers' division." Jake hit the ceiling.

"Vot do you mean, Greenfield's idea? Hipple told me about it a month ago."

"O.K. Jake," the sales manager laughed, "Greenfield told us he got it from Hipple. Now let's use them." We did. We got more mileage out of those dice than the law allows. It was the little extra zinger that sparked a great promotion.

The nice thing about merchandising is that anyone can think up better-than-average ways to promote his product if he really puts on his thinking cap. As Voltaire said, "No problem can stand the assault of sustained thinking."

Here's a good example of applying the grey matter. Fedders came out with a program one season called "T.N.T." We ran full-page ads in *Life* and *Saturday Evening Post* telling the public we were going to give away 2,000 Fedders air conditioners free. You wouldn't have to buy anything; just take the coupon into your local dealer and see if he had your winning number. Come in and see "Penny Penguin." We had cardboard displays of penguins, banners, you name it.

One of our district managers went into the Sterling Linder department store in Cleveland, Ohio, and talked with the buyer and merchandising manager. Department stores don't give up free window space with ease, but our district manager had a merchandising idea that would make Sterling Linder stick out head and shoulders above the other Cleveland department stores, and above all the rest of the Fedders dealers.

He would purchase two live penguins, and Sterling Linder could put them in their best corner window. They would do a whole North Pole scene. A couple of Fedders units would be running in the window to keep the penguins cool. The more he talked, the more they listened. The district manager told them they could announce that Sterling Linder would donate the penguins to the Cleveland City Zoo after the promotion. It was a riot! At one time the only problem Sterling Linder had was, what happened if the people jamming up against the window broke it? Everyone was asking, have you seen the two penguins down in the

Sterling Linder window? The department store did something they had never done before: set up a fedders display to see as you got off each escalator. Result: Sterling Linder reported they sold more Fedders air conditioners out of season than they had the entire previous season.

And so it goes; "Unusual action creates unusual results!"

Years ago a friend of mine told me he picked up a young fellow who worked for Lucky Strike cigarettes. His car had stalled and my friend was taking him to a gas station to get help. He asked the young man what he did. He replied he worked for American Tobacco Company selling Lucky Strikes. He also told my friend that he was supposed to see all prospects and old accounts and put on his little act, as he called it.

His act was taking out a small bunson burner, putting a little tobacco on a plate attached, and explaining to the dealer how Luckies were better because they were toasted. My friend asked him if he did it on every call. The young man said, "Funny thing is I get an order every place I do it." That little merchandising display was the attention getter—the hold the salesman had while he got the chance to tell his story in a dramatic way.

Just a little lift out of the ordinary will do the trick. When I was sales manager of Ampro Corporation's tape recorder division, I introduced the first window display in that field. I had a window with the tape recorders beautifully displayed. Then I took a couple of rolls of recording tape, strung them all through the display, and put a sign in the window inviting people to guess how many feet of tape were in the window and win a free tape recorder. I got the window at a good traffic location and the support of the dealer because I was trying to do a little more than just transfer the place of storage.

Here is how I tell it to my audiences:

"Did you ever wonder *why* you're eating pork sausage some morning? I'll tell you why. About four in the afternoon your wife was at the supermarket shopping. She was tired and hungry. A young lady came up to her with a tray and offered her a piece of perfectly-cooked pork sausage on a stick. Your wife was drooling and said, "Yes." The next morning you're eating pork sausage! They don't have to have that young lady in the supermarket merchandising that pork sausage. They do it because it increases the sale of the sausage.

I watched a young lady behind the counter of a Lincoln music store in New York selling records. They weren't all sealed up like they are today. Everytime someone came up to her with a record they had selected she would take it out of its jacket, reach over and pick up a can and spray the record and place it back in the jacket. She never said a word to the customer. But every customer I watched said, "What's that?"

Then for the first time she said, "Oh, it's called 'Static Free.' It keeps dust and lint off your record. The sound is better and the record lasts longer." She then went about ringing up the sale. The next time she spoke was to tell the customer the price of a can of "Static Free." Out of twenty-six record sales I watched, seventeen of them also bought "Static Free." Leave out the demonstration and the way the young lady handled it, and she'd be lucky to sell six out of twenty-six.

It's confirmed. If you are of average build, you have sixty-six pounds of muscle and three ounces of brains in your body. The odds against your making it with muscle are pretty slim, but you can with the three ounces of brains. It's very much like a muscle in one way. The more you use it, the bigger and better it gets. So don't ever miss the chance to turn that three ounces of brains loose on merchandising the product you're selling.

WHAT YOU CAN DO TO SELL YOURSELF RICH:

1. This chapter you've just read is packed with merchandising ideas that paid big dividends for real live people who used them.
2. I have never seen a product whose sales can't be enhanced by merchandising designed to get and hold a prospective customer's attention.
3. Today! Work out some new merchandising methods to help you do a better job for your company, plus use the ones your company has already been trying to get you to use.

Get in on the Big Sell

Chapter 11

1. What Goethe had to say about your success or failure.
2. How to use the "Big Sell" cards. A warning: If you try and use them all at one time you'll fail. Take them one at a time and you'll do a better job at whatever you're doing.

ON THE NEXT PAGE YOU'LL SEE the front cover of a folder that holds eight cards.* And on the following page you'll see the inside cover that holds the cards, and a quotation you can live by all the days of your life. The more you read it the more you will realize how it applies to anyone's life—anyone's!

Bring Goethe's saying up to date and it would go like this:

"Lose this day goofing off and you'll do the same tomorrow—a ball game, a movie or a little golf. Then pretty soon you'll begin to wonder what the hell is happening; start worrying over the goofed-off time and your job.

"Do you really want more money, a promotion? Then go man, go! What you can do or think you can do is half the battle. Boldness has the edge, the power and the magic. Unusual action gets unusual results. As soon as you begin in earnest the mind grows heated; and if you stick to it, the job will be completed!"

When I was selling I'd no more go out of the house without those eight cards than I'd go out without my pants on. Now you can get in on THE BIG SELL!

Selling is No. 1 and will be until the end of time—never forget, until someone sells something, nothing happens. I need no bookkeepers, no trucks, no credit managers, no shipping department, no anything!—until THE BIG SELL. What part do *you* play?

*These cards have been reproduced as sales aids and are available from the publisher, Acropolis Books Ltd., 2400 17th Street, N.W., Washington, D.C. 20009, in quantities of 12 for $10—postpaid. Please send payment with order.

53

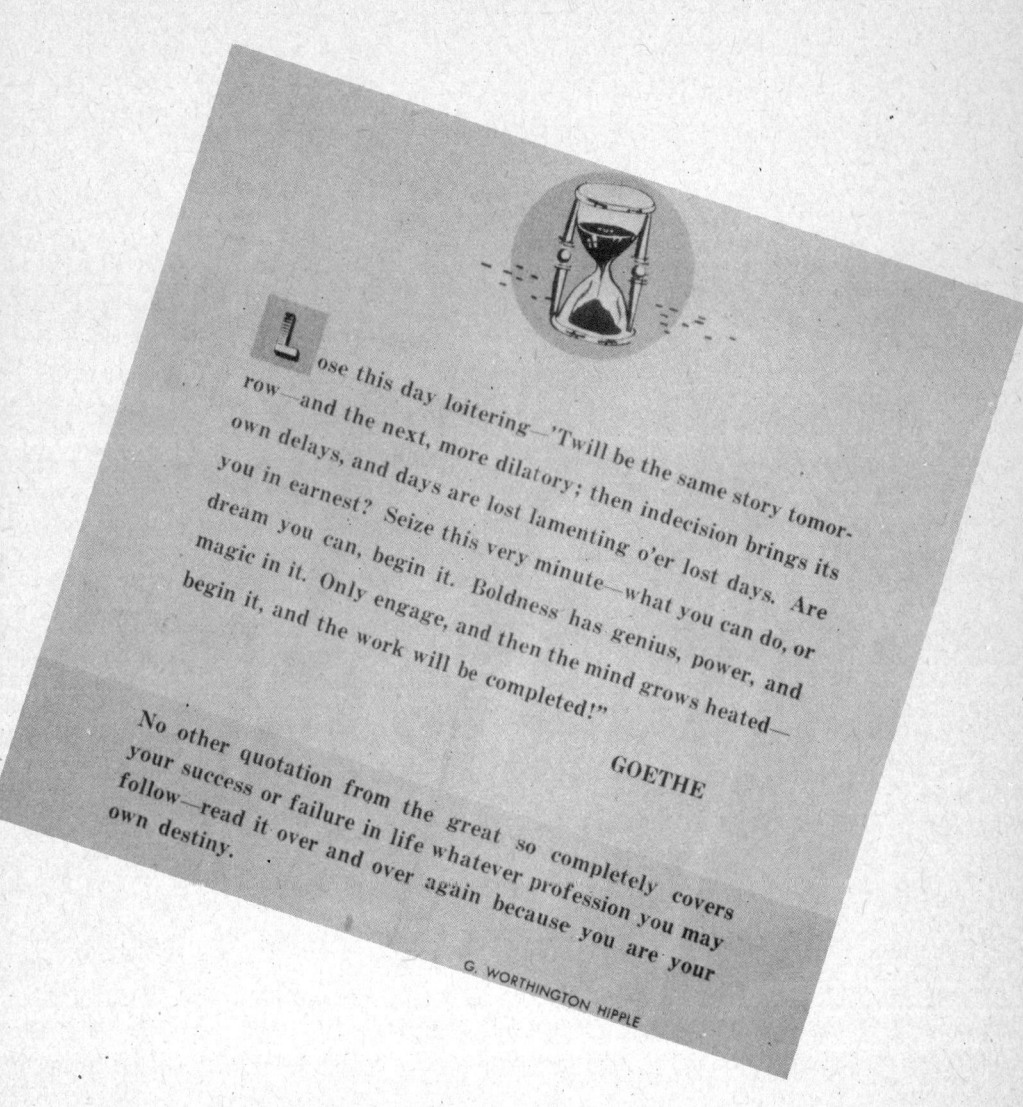

This is the inside cover of the jacket that holds the eight cards on the following pages. It's a good capsule reminder to keep selling yourself rich!

"If you wanna get business you gotta make calls"

There are few salesmen alive who haven't seen the above on some calling card, at some time. It's corny (you'll never find it on the card of any giant corp.—they'd never stoop to such methods) yet it's so basic, so fundamental in selling that it must **FOREVER BE FIRST!** All else follows.

I once had a salesman working for me who had a lot of strikes against him and he actually had the poorest territory, but in all the contests we had, out of twenty-two salesmen, he was always in the top three. He stuck with the corny method . . . made more calls. If the average was forty-eight—he made ninety-six. His favorite expression was, "I can match any salesman's ten o'clock call with an eight o'clock call."

If you can't follow through almost 100% on the above—save your eyes. Don't read about the "Big Sell." May I suggest you give up—go into some other profession, anything but not selling.

SELL YOURSELF RICH

If I could will you one great asset it would be **enthusiasm**! Play it safe and double the enthusiasm you're now using. Enthusiasm is the most contagious selling disease in the world. Remember the old bromide, "Laugh and the world laughs with you—cry and you cry alone."—It's the same with enthusiasm. Think of your hobby* and apply that same zeal and enthusiasm to your selling. You'll double your ability and income. Memorize and sear into your brain, William Randolph Hearst's expression: "If you want the public to get excited about your product—First get excited about it yourself."

*If you haven't got one, get one.

NUMBER 1

SELL YOURSELF RICH

A great man once said, "Considering that in conversation knowledge was obtained rather by the use of THE EARS than THE TONGUE, I gave SILENCE second place among the virtues I determined to cultivate."

My dad told me, "The mind is like a one car garage, you can't put another car in until you take the other car out."

Silence! while your customer or friend takes his car out. You'll be surprized and amazed how easy it is to slip yours in by being the great listener at the right time. Look him straight in the face and listen with all your attention and never expect more than you give.

NUMBER 2

SELL YOURSELF RICH

Hubbard said, "If you want to get something done—ask the man who's busy—he'll have time."

Busy men—successful men—organize! They plan their work and then work their plan.

Tell the average man, "Clean up this warehouse!" and most will reply, "Where shall I start?" Tell the same man, "Put all the Radios on the west wall and all the ranges on the south wall, etc." He'll do the job in jig time, because someone else organized his thinking and working. Learn to do it yourself. Can you make more money? Certainly—you might even own the place some day. You can either follow or lead. The decision is yours. Leaders can and do organize.

NUMBER 3

SELL YOURSELF RICH

Ask yourself, deep down in your heart—"How much genuine knowledge do I have of what I sell?"

You go to a specialist (pay more and like it) because he has more knowledge in his particular field than does the average person.
An average person makes average pay.

Men ask me, "where did you learn so much about selling?" In a nice way I reply, "not from watching T.V. or reading the sports page. I search for selling knowledge where selling knowledge is."

Every selling product has a trade journal—do you read it? Treat yourself to Fortune Magazine and Advertising Age. Read them from cover to cover, you're in for a shock if you do. Soon you'll find you're able to talk on an intelligent level with the buyers you call on—they'll like it—you'll sell more.

NUMBER 4

SELL YOURSELF RICH

"Weak persons cannot be sincere," quote Rochefoucauld. Nor can a man produce results for any given length of time if he is not sincere.

Sincere people have such an advantage over their fellow man. They don't have to remember everything they say. You can't afford anything but sincerity in selling—nobody gets rich on a one shot sale. A sincere effort in selling shines like the sun—through all the years. When you're selling and make that closing point—remember there is nothing as truthful as the truth.

NUMBER 5

SELL YOURSELF RICH

"I remember the face—but I can't remember the name!" That line can destroy you.

A good friend of mine asked a leading psychologist at a large university—"Professor, why is it I can't remember people's names?" The professor replied instantly, "Glen, the real reason you can't remember names is—you just don't give a damn!" And how about you? It's one of the greatest assets in dealing with people and you know it!

Use the oldest and best method for remembering—Association. How many times have you heard your wife, mother or yourself remember or establish some date **years back** by association? "It was the year Paul and Helen got married and that was ten years ago—so the house is eleven years old."

Say "I **will**—not I'll try" to remember—Remember people's names!—Make it a **must**!

NUMBER 6

SELL YOURSELF RICH

Doesn't the photographer always say, "SMILE PLEASE?" You'll look better, you'll feel better, you'll sell better, **when you smile.** You don't have to be a laughing boy, but smile and let it come from within. People like to do business with affable people. They smile and tell a pleasant story.

You get what you put out—A smile begets a smile—A frown begets a frown and if pushed far enough a punch in the nose begets a punch in the nose.

Too many of us save a smile for a select few. Give it a fair trial—smile at all the little people through life that you hadn't reserved a smile for in the past.

You can win with 7 and get in on, "THE BIG SELL."

NUMBER 7

What's on these cards is what most salesmen blow most of the time. Either they don't know it, or know it but don't put it into practice on every call. Remember, don't slip up on the basics.

WHAT YOU CAN DO TO SELL YOURSELF RICH:

1. If you try to use the cards all at one time, you'll fail. Take them one at a time, and you'll be a winner. Practice one card conscientiously for a day at a time until they all become second nature to you.
2. Read Goethe's saying, then read it again, then read it again, then ACT!

You Can't Sell Peanuts at the End of the Parade

Chapter 12

1. See if you are as smart as a fourteen-year-old farm boy.
2. How do you match up against a New York peanut vendor?
3. Don't pass up another day without preparing for tomorrow.

I USED THAT THEME for one of the national conventions I keynoted for Fedders Corporation some years ago. You'll remember I've told you you can only take out of any situation what you put into it. For that convention I had a company make me up 436 bags of peanuts with "You can't sell peanuts at the end of the parade" on each bag in red letters. Then I went out and hired a peanut vendor who worked the sidewalks of New York. I paid him $20 to appear at a rehearsal and $20 to stand on the stage with his peanut cart through my whole presentation.

Most air conditioning companies need their sales people like a hole in the head during June, July and August. When they need us is during January, February, March and April. If we haven't done our work by then, we're dead. And in September, October and November the parade is over. The same thing is true of so many businesses that have a seasonal product. It's too bad more merchants, even big businesses don't think like a farmer.

I can still hear my uncle telling his son, "Jesse, I want you to go out and plow that hundred and ten acres west of the creek. After you've finished the plowing we'll have to use the disk and the harrow; then we'll be ready for the seeding." Jesse was ready to walk out when my uncle said, "Not so fast, Jess. After that crop gets up we'll have to do some cultivating, then maybe some

The old peanut vendor knew he couldn't sell peanuts at the end of the parade.

spraying, and God willin', if we get the rain and sun, we'll have ourselves a good crop."

Jesse might not be the brightest kid in the world, but he does everything his pa tells him. Result? Every year the crop gets bigger, and the funny thing about it is that Jesse never tries to mastermind it as we city slickers do. He never thinks, "Maybe I can leave the plowing out. I'll just break the ground up with the harrow. Or, I'll put the seeds in, but I'll leave the cultivating out." Year in and year out he follows the same tried and true routine. And he always gets a crop.

If you go out and buy a lot of merchandise in June to sell in November or December, you'd better get your house in order. If you sell a lot of merchandise to a retailer customer of yours and you don't want the parade to pass him by, you'd better take a lesson from the peanut vendor. He's got those peanuts bagged, displayed and his cart out on the street long before the parade starts. The old peanut vendor told me, "You gotta catch 'em when they're hot; not too many people buying when the parade is over."

If you just sell 'em and let it go at that, you're going to be looking at a customer who has some leftover merchandise when you show up to get the next order. As a salesman, you have got to do a lot more than just transfer the place of storage.

It's really true of almost all businesses. Here's an example that might surprise you:

A young man who is manager of a large Quality Inn in Louisville, Kentucky, told me this story of how he didn't try to sell peanuts at the end of the parade. I was a consultant to Quality Inns at the time, and he had him come up to tell his story at one of the Quality Inn national conventions. And brother, take it from me, it applies to your business as much as the motel business.

What did he have to sell? Rooms. When was his big parade? Every time they ran the Kentucky Derby, and they've been running it for seventy-five years. You're already thinking, how much selling do you have to do when all those people are pouring into Louisville looking for a room? Not much if you're a gambler. Here's the package the manager had ready in January for the Derby:

Every registered guest gets a free ticket to the Derby. When you get to your room there is a bottle of Kentucky bourbon on your table with your name printed on the bottle. The manager bought a Tennessee Walking Horse that he paid $1500 for. Every guest received a chance to win the horse. He had a bus to take the guests to and from the Derby. He was sold out of all of his rooms at $40 a day before the horses ever arrived at the track. High price for the room? The people didn't think so. He turned away enough guests to fill another motel the size of his. He could have left all his special services out and taken a chance on being filled to capacity at $20 or $22.50 a day.

So be sure when you sell any customer of yours you show him a way to get ready for the parade—*before* it comes down the street. Do you want to know what I used to tell my customers in the air conditioning business?

"Sam, I don't want you to sign this order if you're not going to use this direct mail campaign in March and April, if you're not going to use this window display of ours, if you're not going to tie in with our national advertising, if your salesmen are not going to make follow-up calls on the leads we will be furnishing." So help me, for a moment he'd look at me as if I wasn't quite right in the head. And if that wasn't enough, before he could say anything I'd also tell him, "You can't do it with one or two models. You've got to use our display stand (and heaven help him if I ever found any other brand in our Fedders display stand). It'll give you a good cross-section of our line." When I finished explaining why I wanted Sam to do all those things, touch all those bases, even old hardheaded Sam got the message. I wasn't interested in just transferring the place of storage, of taking back any of what I sold him.

As I told you, the parade is over come September, October, November and December in the air conditioning business. It's like trying to sell a Valentine card in August. Be prepared.

WHAT YOU CAN DO TO SELL YOURSELF RICH:

1. There is a planting season.
2. There is a cultivating time.
3. There is a time to bring in the sheaves.
4. The farming system above applies 1000 percent to selling of any kind.

Time Is Silent and Deadly

Chapter 13

1. Time can be your own worst enemy.
2. How to use precious minutes to improve yourself.
3. Organizing yourself is the first step in saving time.

"THOSE THAT DARE LOSE A DAY, are dangerously prodigal; those that dare mis-spend it, are desperate."—B. P. Hall

If Hall is right, I've met thousands upon thousands of desperate men in my life.

You can wind up as a quiet failure by abusing time. Time has to be our worst enemy. He won't stand up and fight like a man. He won't give you a warning, even a little one like, "Hey, fellow, you just blew another minute." A minute! Perhaps you think I'm cutting it a little too fine. But take a good look:

THE HIGH COST OF A MISSING MINUTE:

To show what those precious four hours of selling time per day are made of, this table gives the worth to you of each 60-second interval. If your annual earnings are:

$6,000, every minute is worth $.10, or a phone call
$9,000, "   "   "   " $.15, or a newspaper
$12,000, "   "   "   " $.20, or two postage stamps
$15,000, "   "   "   " $.25, or half a loaf of bread
$20,000, "   "   "   " $.33, or a little more than half a gallon of gas
$25,000, "   "   "   " $.42, or half a dozen eggs

(Updated from *How to Get More Done in Less Time*, by Joseph D. Cooper)

A book you should run out and buy and read from cover to cover is *How to Get More Done in Less Time*, by Joseph D. Cooper. He covers every aspect of time. The book is easy-to-read and understandable. So get it.

Here is another little question that makes you think, from Cooper's book. He asks you what it's worth to save a single hour in a day, on the average. In a normal lifetime, one hour saved each day of a five-day week is worth six years! Six productive years. What would you do if I could grant you a wish—if I could make you thirty instead of thirty-six; forty-nine years old instead of fifty-five; fifty-nine instead of social security age? What would you do if I sentenced you to six solid years in the penitentiary with no time off for good behavior?

And to think that one lousy little hour taking a nap or watching the idiot box cheats you out of six whole productive years of your life.

Have you ever wondered what you could do with an hour towards bettering yourself? An hour? How about fifteen minutes? I heard the late Dale Carnegie tell an audience in New York City that if you read all you could find out about whales for fifteen minutes a day, you would soon be one of the three or four top authorities on whales. Maybe you don't want to be an authority on whales. How about being an authority on the field you're in? How about being a man or woman who can fit in almost anyplace with well-educated people? Complete the "Great Books" course, all fifty-four volumes. They tell you it is for the average man who hates being average. When you've finished the "Great Books," you'll be as well-read—perhaps more so—as a person with a master's degree from any university in the country. In just fifteen minutes a day you can go from Sigmund Freud to Boswell to Homer and back again.

It must be frightening to millions of men watching the pro football games on TV. The owner of the Pittsburg pro team walked out with only twenty-five seconds remaining when his team was playing the Oakland Raiders for the right to play the winner of the Miami-Cleveland game. In that twenty-five seconds Pittsburgh came from behind and won the game. You could have had a cardiac arrest in 1971 watching old George Blanda pull one game after the other out of the fire for the Raiders. One with twelve seconds left, and one right down to four seconds. Man, wouldn't it be something if all salesmen learned to nurse their time like a pro quarterback nurses a minute or less!

If you understood where your time went; *if* you applied what they call the first rule: organize yourself; *if* you saved all the time that you could by looking ahead—then you would multiply yourself by the right use of your time. You can do it, but I'm the first to admit we have to go back to the words of Cal Coolidge. It's going to take some of that persistence he talked about that you've got buried inside.

You could start by cutting out your coffee breaks, not all of them. If you did that, you could take a four-year leave of absence.

This is going to hurt. Granted it's only my observation, but I've watched it closely. I never see the winners, the ones who make it big, with a cup of coffee in their hands every few minutes. It's always the little people. I will never if I live to be a hundred forget a scene at the home office of Fedders when we were in Maspeth, New York. I had been called in for a meeting and arrived at the office as the office personnel were taking their places. At nine o'clock a young kid came around, and I saw him going from desk to desk with a pad writing down what the various people wanted to consume on company time. "I'll have my coffee black." Make mine the same with sugar, and one Danish." This went on for about fifteen minutes. Thirty-five minutes later the kid was back with the orders. Another fifteen to twenty minutes went by as he dished out the right thing to each worker ant. Now! Now we stop whatever we're doing and eat. It's not a union rest period; it's the little people thinking it's their God-given right to have one breakfast at home and another one at the office. But if you ask the average employee about his work that has piled up, he'll tell you, "I just don't have enough time."

Soon I was called into the president's office. I couldn't find one cup of coffee or a piece of Danish.

"Improve your opportunities," said Napoleon to a school of young men; "*Every hour lost now* is a chance of future failure."

(See Next Page for What You Can Do to Sell Yourself Rich)

WHAT YOU CAN DO TO SELL YOURSELF RICH:

1. Now you know the high cost of a minute: Be sure and get Cooper's book on time.
2. Give yourself a break today and every other day. Take one hour a day to increase your total self.
   a. You could take an accounting course.
   b. An advertising course.
   c. A speaking course.
   d. A typing course.
   e. A language course.

   Don't cop out. Even if you live in East Podunk, you can get involved in any of the above. If you can't go in person, you can take a correspondence course.
3. How valuable do you think you would be compared to the other men in the company if in three years you did the following:

   1st year: you took the Dale Carnegie speaking course.

   2nd year: you took a bookkeeping or accounting course.

   3rd year: you took some other course that closely fit the work you do for your company.

   And if you kept it up? Some day you'd be the president of your company.

Come in, Said the Spider to the Fly

Chapter 14

1. Are you really of value to your customer, or just an order taker?
2. Do you know how many people in a company can have a hand in your making a sale?
3. What buyers like and dislike about salesmen.

PICTURE A STERN-FACED MAN with a cigar clamped tightly between his teeth. He's looking straight at you and says the following:
 I don't know who you are.
 I don't know your company.
 I don't know your company's objectives.
 I don't know your company's reputation.
 I don't know your company's service reliability.
 I don't know if I can depend on you.
 I don't know if you can help me.
 Now, what was it you wanted to sell me?

That's for openers. Now if you're ready for him, just maybe he'll be ready for you.

Here is how W. A. MacCalla, Supervisor of Industrial Sales of West Penn Power Company, suggests you use sales aids and promotional material to pre-sell.

Actually, no introduction is needed for the stern-faced buyer with the cigar clamped tightly in his mouth. You know this man. He's a customer. *Your* customer may not look like this guy, but he'll have the same icy stare and maybe he, too, will say, "I don't know who you are. I don't know your company," etc. Sometimes he may say nothing, but he'll be communicating, all right. The problem is *this* man really *doesn't* know you. He may be a new customer. Maybe he's a vice president or chief engineer from the home office, or perhaps a new plant manager. Maybe he came up through the ranks so fast he was overlooked as a future buying influence. It's possible that his company, once small, suddenly mushroomed, and because of the many demands on your time, you were unable to get around and see him.

How do you avoid meeting this man? You don't. You seek him out as early as possible. You have a pre-selling job to do—gaining his friendship, his respect, and his confidence in you and your company. You do this because it is a well-known fact that people—yes, even so-called hard-headed businessmen, prefer to do business with those they know and like the best.

At this point you may be thinking, "Why start a presentation on pre-selling by talking about people?" That's because it's important to recognize that we sell *people* not companies. Extensive studies show that industrial executives, managers, engineers, or purchasing agents are motivated to buy services and supplies by essentially the same hopes and fears, needs and ambitions that lead them to buy their favorite brands of toothpaste, razor, automobile, yacht, or house. In short, the industrial buyer is more human in his buying habits than marketers realize.

Today's successful salesman must have, among other skills, the ability to put himself in the customer's shoes, understand his needs and feelings. He knows that every sale involves a choice, and that the buyer needs assurance that he is making the right choice. He must get to the buyer by *demonstrating that his knowledge and ability can be of value to the customer*. When his confidence is earned and maintained, the way is paved for sales.

There are many ways of getting established with customer people. If you've been assigned a new account, there's no better way possible than to get a personal introduction by the salesman who previously had the account. If it's a new out-of-town headquarters contact, get an official of the local plant to prepare the way. Participation with customers on industry associations, technical committees, and civic affairs is another good way of getting to know a customer better. And be sure to take advantage of requests to speak at meetings attended by your customers, for they'll recognize you as an expert, or specialist, in your subject.

So far, we've been considering the customer as an individual person. But of course there aren't many one-man companies anymore! So the job is to identify with *all* the people who influence the specifying and purchasing of equipment you sell.

Rarely is one man the *only* one in his company involved in a purchase. How many people do you have to see to make a sale? *Factory* magazine made a study of two companies, each with a few thousand employees, to determine exactly how many people were involved in purchases of industrial equipment and services. One company was Century Electric in St. Louis. The other was Yale and Towne in Philadelphia. The study showed that in the Century plant, there were thirty-nine people with buying influence; at Yale and Towne there were sixty. Between eight and twelve men were involved in an average purchasing decision. The study also showed that salesmen reached only 16.5 percent of those with buying influence at Century, and only 11.27 percent at Yale and Towne.

Chemical Engineering magazine reported that their study showed that a majority of people who specify and buy industrial products and services never see a salesman.

But being a flea-bitten power salesman with over thirty years of experience behind me I thought, "Well, those figures are all right for those who are selling lighting fixtures, circuit breakers, machine tools, and other such products. But we're different." *Sure* we are! We don't sell nuts and bolts, pots and pans. We sell concepts, such as electric process heating, automation, year-round air conditioning, etc. We're also a kind of privileged group. We rarely have to sit around, hat in hand, in a purchasing agent's office. We're known by the plant guard at the gate and get right in to see the plant engineer, the works engineer, the works manager, and when need be, the owner or top executive.

Sure, we're different! And to prove it I talked to some of our most experienced salesmen who call on plants the same size as the ones surveyed by *Factory*. One thing they all agreed on was the more contacts you have from the top to the bottom, the better your chances of a sale.

We could travel faster, fight harder and pound louder on the customer's door. It would bring some results, but they would tend to be short-term. In our fast-moving, fast-growing economy companies are finding you can't play man-to-man coverage. So we use another aid.

Let's look at the individual parts of a coordinated program to get in touch, and keep in touch, with customers. Let's consider how you can use the printed word as a communication channel to help make sales. By "printed word," I mean publications, direct mail, promotional brochures, clippings, and reprints. If you've noticed that I've shied away from using the word *advertising*, it's only because of my fear of being lynched by those few old-time uncompromising men who still feel the power sales profession's dignity, their status, and perhaps even their job is threatened by advertising. Of course nothing could be further from the truth. Instead, it's the mark of a skillful and prudent salesman to use advertising and other promotional material to help pre-sell.

Advertising can't personalize customer relations, make an engineering or feasibility study, or get a contract signed.

On the other hand, advertising *can* do many things very effectively and efficiently:
1. It can call on the man you never or rarely see.
2. It can *call consistently* on individuals with whom you have limited contact. And don't be timid about sending direct mail to your customers' top people.
3. It can do a softening up job, a pre-sell job on your customer before you call. [Author's note: Someone once said, "There is nothing as powerful as the printed word—you can't talk back or argue with it."]
4. Last but not least, don't ever forget that engineers, plant managers and buyers are as susceptible to all forms of advertising as you and I.

Well, we now have a good account of how industrial salesmen should handle themselves in their type of selling and how they, like those in any other business, must take advantage of the weight of advertising. It's well to heed Mr. MacCalla's advice in handling industrial customers, but also heed all the advice you can get, whatever your product is.

We aren't very well-liked by most buyers. Here is what 1,000 buyers had to say about what they liked and disliked about salesmen who called on them. How do you rate?

DISLIKED:
1. Didn't know his business
2. Never brought an idea with him
3. Knocked his competition
4. Talked too much
5. Poor presentation
6. Did a lot of crying about how bad business was
7. Talked about his personal problems

LIKED:
1. Makes friends (but not too buddy-buddy)
2. Handles complaints with disptach and follows through
3. Knows his goods and has back-up confirmation
4. Has a good appearance
5. Keeps his personal problems to himself
6. Has an earnest desire to see that we move his goods after taking the order

As Bill Gove says in his talk, "Don't Be Plate-Glass Shy":
"Too many salesmen like to call on a mom and pop account but panic when they have to call on the big boys."

Some years ago I met a man by the name of Dave Harris who ran a very large distributing house, very, very successfully. Here is what he told me: "If I ever hear of one of my salesmen asking a customer how business is, I'll fire him. If you ask a customer how business is, most of them will tell you and then justify it by not giving you an order."

When buyers talk about what they like about salesmen they mention appearance. One large insurance company uses this little touch to remind their men to look well groomed when they go out for the day. As you leave the office you pass a large full-length mirror with a sign over it that says: "Do you look your best?"

Let's remember Lincoln's sage remark, "When you can't remove an obstacle, plow around it." But you can make your obstacle look a lot less formidable by doing your homework in advance, and by pre-selling the customer.

WHAT YOU CAN TO TO SELL YOURSELF RICH:

1. You must be able to put yourself in the buyer's shoes. <u>Understand</u> his needs.
2. Be sure you know and identify with all the people involved in making a sale in every company you are trying to do business with. And never forget the little people.
3. Soften up your client. Use all the pre-sell at your disposal.
4. Take a good, hard look at yourself. How do you rate on the checklist? How can you make the "liked" list?

Chapter 15

You Can't Do It Alone

---

1. The best have failed trying to do it alone.
2. Never sell short the corny word "teamwork."
3. How the winners do it.

YOU'VE GOT TO USE ALL THE AVAILABLE help around you. There's plenty of it. First let me convince you that teamwork is the secret—teamwork helps in your selling just as it does in sports.

This is a true story. Wilt Chamberlain, the great basketball player, used to play with Philadelphia. He was at his peak when he was playing against the great Boston Celtics in the Eastern Division.

There was one thing all pros in basketball would bet on. No man would ever score 100 points in one game. Now think about that for a moment. Certainly a superhuman effort would be required. Right? Right.

Wilt Chamberlain did it. He scored 100 points in one game. Yet in all the time he played for Philadelphia they never won a championship. If you don't already know, I'll tell you who won all the championships so many years in a row it became monotonous. Boston. Did any one on the Boston Celtics score 100 points, or even 75 points? No. You saw that their winning score was spread around about like this: 28, 22, 20, 17, 24. And they just kept winning with Havlicek, Russell, Jones, Jones and Cousy.

I had those film clips dug out of that basketball game in which "Wilt The Stilt" scored his 100 points. Then I had the

75

company that had the film also splice on some footage showing the Green Bay Packers in action with Paul Horning and Taylor running. It was a symphony watching the great Paul Horning in action. To watch him you'd think he was doing a slow foxtrot to the local pub. He was perfection loping along behind his blockers. Lombardi said, "Horning never tried to do it alone. It was one of his many outstanding traits."

I've seen more sales people trying to do it alone—on their connections, their looks, on their charm, on just making more calls. It never quite comes off. It's when you put it all together. You've listened to "teamwork" so long it's a wonder you're not ready to throw up. But still, many of us violate this concept in almost everything we do.

I had a young man working for me as a district manager. As Hugh Marlowe said, "Everybody is two people—the one we see and the one inside." On the outside my district manager was a world-beater—really good looking, well built, a good speaking voice and very personable. I finally discovered he could do most of his business, what he did, over the phone. He had every secretary of every distributor in his back pocket. But advertising, merchandising, promotion were all left to chance. Very few people in life have the headstart, the advantages, this young man had. If he had wanted to work instead of loaf there was no limit to the heights he could have scaled. I found out by chance after we let him go that he had made it through college the same way he had tried to sell. He had used his good looks and charm. A fellow who went to school with him said there wasn't a co-ed in the school that wasn't willing to sit up all night to write a term paper for him. It may have worked in college, but it didn't work out in the real world.

When you're not using your advertising to its fullest, your promotional material to its fullest, the credit department to its fullest, your service department to its fullest, and the personnel at your home office to their fullest, you're trying to do it alone.

Instead, use every asset you can lay your hands on. Pay attention—they're all around you.

A LATE FLASH:

I was watching on TV the Los Angeles Lakers professional basketball team play the Milwaukee Bucks. During a time out the announcer remarked, "So far Milwaukee hasn't beat the Lakers this season, although their star, Abdul Jabbar, has scored the most points on both teams in all three games. His trouble seems to be he hasn't had much help from his supporting cast."

A nice up-to-date way of saying, "You can't do it alone."

WHAT YOU CAN DO TO SELL YOURSELF RICH:

1. Use your advertising department to its fullest.
2. Be on good terms and work with your credit department.
3. Keep those ears open. Listen to how some of your fellow salesmen may have cracked a client with their approach.
4. We all need all the help we can get. Remember what Woodrow Wilson said: "I use all the knowledge I have and borrow all that I can."
5. Don't expect to get along on your good looks and charm.

Don't Get Too Technical   Chapter 16

1. You could lose the sale.
2. A classic example of how to sell—it hasn't changed in over sixty years.
3. Sell it for what it will do for the customer.
4. Watch how you say it and when you say it. They used to call it "death" insurance. Now they call it "LIFE" insurance.

SELL IT FOR WHAT IT WILL DO for the customer. Just about everything in selling has been tried before. There's not much new, just variations. You can still learn from the classics, and think up your own variations.

Let me tell you a true, classic story of how one of the great American salesmen sold the first automobiles in the United States.

He worked for a company most of you have never heard of. It was the Chalmers Motor Car Company and the time was circa 1912.

The man was my father, George W. Hipple. When he was quite old he used to say to me, "Worthington, did I ever tell you how I first started selling cars?" He had, but I'd always say, "No." I wanted to hear it again so I'd never forget it. Here it is:

"The president of the Chalmers Motor Car Company decided to open their first show room in Chicago, Illinois. They sent two engineers and me to Chicago. The idea was that I could tell the engineers about selling and they could tell me about the technical end of the car."

I was always a good straight man and said, "How did it work out?"

"Well, not long after we were open, I was standing behind a pillar watching the engineers trying to sell one of the cars to a prospect who had come into the show room. They took the man up to the front of the car and said, 'This is the crank; you want to be sure and hold the handle like this so it doesn't kick back and break your arm. Now come over here by the steering wheel. If the lights start to dim you use this pump here.' Then they opened the door and one of them got in. 'If the car stalls you lift up the floor boards right here and flip this lever over to the left. Now, come back here.' And they went to the back of the car and one of them got down on the floor. 'You can take this plate off back here on the axle and by just. . .' " My father said it wasn't long before the customer was gone.

I asked, "How did you sell them?"

"I had a car parked in front of the showroom on Michigan Boulevard. It took a lot of nerve in those days to even come in and look over one of those horseless carriages. As soon as a looker came in I said, 'Let's go outside. I have a car in front of the showroom.'

"When we got out there I told the looker to get in. He would start to get in on the seat next to the driver's side. I'd tell him to get in behind the wheel and he'd look at me wide-eyed and exclaim, 'Me?, I couldn't drive one of these.'

" 'How'd you get over here?' I'd ask," my father continued.

" 'In my buggy,'

" 'It's the same as driving your buggy. When you want to go to the right, what do you do? You pull the reins to the right. When you want to go to the left, you pull them to the left. When you want to stop, you pull back on the reins and plant your feet down on the buckboard. You just hold the steering wheel and push down on those two pedals. Get in.'

"Pretty soon I'd have that car going down Michigan Boulevard with that man behind the wheel. We'd be going about twelve miles an hour. In those days you didn't have to worry about anyone hitting you; everybody got out of your way. That man had hold of that steering wheel so tightly only God could have taken it out of his hands. All the time I'd be telling him how he could drive out in the country with the family. I never did tell him if he went more than a couple of miles on the roads we had then he'd probably have to get a team of horses to bring him back. That night he'd go home the owner of a Chalmers Motor Car and say to his wife, 'Mary, I bought one of them new fangled automobiles today!' "

I asked him with a grin, "Wasn't that kind of sneaky selling?"

"No, not really. Once he had committed himself, then it was easy to tell him about some of the things the engineers were telling their prospects right off the bat."

It's been true of new products since the beginning of time. If you want to lose a sale, start out by telling the prospect what he has to watch out for!

When I was pioneering TV sales I had the same option. I could use the engineers' approach or my father's.

I could have told the people, "Be sure and don't fool around with the back of the set. There is so much voltage back there you could get killed in a minute. You won't be able to get many stations and the ones you do get won't be very clear. You'll have to have an outside antenna and that will cost you a bundle. They broadcast almost three hours a day now." No sir! First I got them hooked on the idea of keeping up with their neighbors, the prestige of ownership and the fun the whole family would have watching Milton Berle. If I did a good job on that score, they would be the first one to show me where we could put the antenna on the roof.

Nobody ever really cared how the picture on the TV got there. Nobody worried too much about how the air conditioner made the room cool and comfortable. When I think back at all the jazz salesmen used to tell people about air conditioning! I asked my boss once how we got stuck with a particularly poor salesman.

"Oh," he said, "I hired him when we first started. He knows how to take one apart and put it together again."

Don't talk about evaporators, condensers, etc. Talk about the fact that you'll be able to get a good night's sleep when it's ninety-five outside. The fact that you can shut all the windows and have a cleaner house, the fact that maybe Suzie has a sinus condition and the air conditioning will help, or maybe big daddy has a heart condition and during a heat wave an air conditioned room will help him. Sell all that, and they won't worry about that big klunker sticking out of the window. They won't balk at putting in the right kind of wiring.

I realize you must know the cold facts. You must have technical knowledge on thousands of products sold. I just want you to be darn sure you *put them in the right order.* First sell him on the idea, then he'll willingly accept the technical end, even if it hurts.

Don't ever forget my classic line: "Last year one million people bought quarter-inch drills—not because they wanted quarter-inch drills, but because they wanted one million quarter-inch holes!" Sell the people what they want.

WHAT YOU CAN DO TO SELL YOURSELF RICH:

1. Be sure you sell it for what it will do for the customer. If you do they will accept any technical aspect of the product.
2. Keep that old saying uppermost in your mind:
   "Last year one million quarter-inch drills were sold. Not because people wanted one million quarter-inch drills, but because they wanted ONE MILLION QUARTER-INCH HOLES."

How Much Education Do You Need?

Chapter 17

1. How much education do you really need?
2. A curious personnel manager tried to find an occupation that had remained unchanged since World War II. He found only a janitor's job and a handful of assembly line chores.

HERE IS WHAT AN ARTICLE IN THE August 11, 1962, issue of *Business Week* had to say on the subject. After you read it, let's take a look at how times change and see what the same magazine had to say eleven years later about the shift from youth to experience.

"UNTIL RECENTLY, all we asked of a job applicant was that he be able to sign his name and find his way to the time clock. Now he's got to have a high school diploma."

The speaker, a southern California electronics technician, could serve as a spokesman for much of American industry. The high school diploma—once a mark of the better-educated worker and often his passport to a white collar job—has become the minimum requirement for many basic industrial jobs.

A *Business Week* survey of major industrial centers finds the trend toward higher education requirements for factory jobs the strongest in the West Coast aerospace industry (where a high school graduate who has taken high school math courses may start work as a mailboy), weakest in the Southeast's textile and woodworking industries.

In some areas such as Chicago, automation has produced a split trend in companies as diverse as Bell and Howell and United

Biscuit Company. These companies require less than a high school education for the routinized machine operations, more education for trouble shooting jobs.

Overall the trend is up and rising fast. Although some aircraft companies required it twenty years ago, most of the formal requirements for a high school diploma went into effect during the past five years, some within the past two. So did many of the high school-level aptitude requirements, especially in the northern cities with heavy southern migration. And many companies that favor the graduate informally expect to formalize the requirement soon.

The same signs are apparent in apprenticeship programs. Nearly all require a high school diploma, and many require the ability to do college-level work.

The pattern indicates that educationally undemanding companies are often stable or shrinking companies, with few job openings. Growing companies make growing educational demands.

Considered simply as a fact of economic life, the trend toward higher education has the inevitability of Tuesday following Monday.

First of all, galloping technology has made *all jobs* different and harder.

A curious personnel manager recently tried to find an occupation that had remained unchanged since World War II. He tracked down only a janitor's job and a handful of assembly line chores.

A January 6, 1973, *Business Week* article says: "Many top corporations are so hungry for talent that they are even bucking the trend toward youth. So you needn't feel forgotten if you are a middle manager outside the magic 32-to-45 bracket. 'Corporations are placing more emphasis on experience and ability now. They want people who do the job now—not a year from now,' says E. B. Sollis, vice-chairman of Spencer Stuart & Associates."

Well, we know we're pushing water uphill if we choose to make it without the benefit of higher education. What's our next highest card? If we can't go back to college there are many, many ways to add to our knowledge. I took a course on salesmanship at Southeastern University. I've taken the Dale Carnegie course. I faithfully read everything I told you to subscribe to in the chapter titled "Are You Too Busy Chopping Wood to Take Time to Sharpen Your Ax?"

And isn't it nice to know the big corporations are beginning to think like George Allen of the Redskins. He, too, said he wanted experience because he wanted a championship, NOW—not a year from now. So get all the knowledge and experience you can in your job. You could be tapped for something better any day—if you're ready.

WHAT YOU CAN DO TO SELL YOURSELF RICH:

1. Never stop educating yourself.
2. Combine education with experience and you'll be a much sought after salesman.

Are You a Self-Starter?

Chapter 18

1. Being a self-starter takes discipline and character.
2. The constant urge to do better, to accomplish more, is the priceless asset of a truly self-motivated person.
3. Your friends don't really want you to succeed.
4. Voltaire's great one-liner is in this chapter. Use it.
5. If you come up with one great idea in this lifetime, that's all you need. Start thinking.

YOU MAY NOT HAVE BEEN BORN with inner drive, but you can still acquire it. A great mass of salesmen have the same problem they attribute to writers, painters, etc. Not being in an office with a supervisor looking over your shoulder, you can easily start dragging your heels (and the rest of your body). Maybe you have to call in in the morning, and have to send in a daily report, but essentially you are on your own. I used to work with a sales supervisor at Schenley who always had some doubt about the men being on the road in the morning. They had to call in in the morning. During their talk with George Gabor he'd suddenly say, "Jess, I just got an important long distance call. Give me your number and I'll call you right back." Man, you would not believe how many times the salesman gave George his home phone number without realizing it, until it was too late. And George would call him right back.

You can be a self-starter, or follow the other fellow all the way to the bank. It takes discipline and character. Read what Oscar Schisgall has to say on the subject of being a self-starter from an article he wrote for Chicago's *American* magazine.

Pope John XXIII once said, "Often I half-awake at night thinking about a serious problem and decide that I must ask the

Pope what to do about it. Then I wake up completely and remember that I am the Pope."

In two sentences, Pope John pointed out the difference between the responsibilities of those people who must make their own decisions and of those who live by following the decisions of others—in other words, the self-starters and those who are led.

We all want to be considered self-starters; it's a normal bit of egotism. Practically all the pioneering figures who have illuminated history have been self-starters. They earn the rewards, the power, the approbation. But what does it take? What is the magic fuel that sets a person's inner engines to working? In recent months I have been asking psychologists, doctors, business leaders, and educators.

"One thing that marks a self-starter," one psychologist said, "is a desire to satisfy himself—his self-esteem or his conscience. He wants not only the high regard of other people; he must also have his own."

And once he sets himself a course, the truly self-motivated person usually proceeds with the utmost confidence. He has no intention of letting any obstacle stand in his way. When Charles Lindbergh completed the first transatlantic flight, a newspaperman in Paris called out, "Did you ever have any doubts that you'd reach Europe?" Lindbergh grinned and answered, "Do you think I'd have started if I thought I might make it only part-way?"

There are many other common denominators, according to the students of human behavior. Most self-starters, they say, seek the gratification of personal ambition, perhaps of acquiring more luxuries, or of accumulating money, as the primary gauge of a successful life. Others wish to be recognized as leaders. This involves a desire for higher status and the love of public admiration—or even the admiration of some particular person. Some seek the sheer exhilaration of outdoing all competition; everybody likes to win a race. And then there are the fighting crusaders who have only a desire to do what they think is right.

But what we generally applaud in self-starters is the way they seize opportunities that others ignore. This is true not only of the corporation president but also the shoeshine boy who outruns all his competitors in approaching a possible customer. Both have more than energy; they have vision and imagination.

Millions of Americans who have visited France have professed a fondness for French bread. But only one man among all those millions decided to ask the transatlantic airlines if French bread could be delivered to the United States at a reasonable price, and fast enough to be sold the day it was baked. (French bread *must* be eaten fresh.) He was told that loaves brought to Orly airport outside of Paris by 6 a.m. could arrive at Kennedy Airport by 8 a.m. New York time. Trucks meeting the plane could deliver the bread to metropolitan New York food stores within the hour, and connecting flights could carry loaves to other cities within an hour or two.

Today John T. Kuntz is selling French bread daily in more than 40 American cities and reaping his reward. He is living proof of the saying, "Even if the world owes you a living, you have to be your own collector."

Everyone wants to succeed, yet the overwhelming majority of us do not make the effort unless somebody or something supplies us with an external inducement. This fact has given rise to a relatively new and highly specialized vocation: the creation of "incentive programs" in American industry. Such programs offer everything from cash bonuses to automobiles and trips abroad to induce people to work harder, produce more, sell more, earn more. Though these programs usually accomplish their purpose while they last, can they permanently change laggards into self-starters?

"They can and do," says Bernard A. Marden of Marden-Kane, Inc., one of the leaders in the business of devising such programs. "Take the case of the salesman who doubled his business during a six-month company contest and won a trip to Europe. This gave him a taste for foreign travel. He was determined to see other parts of the world. So he set out to earn more to gratify the new desire. By that very effort he became a self-starter."

As Marden suggests, it can be a good thing to give oneself a taste of unaccustomed luxury. If it stimulates work toward higher goals, it can be regarded as an investment. During World War II, Sgt. Milton Hoff was sent to Western Europe's most fashionable spas to arrange care for battle-shocked Army personnel. The spas gave Hoff a taste of luxurious living—and suggested an excellent opportunity. After the war, he borrowed every cent he could and opened a spa of his own. Today his Palm Beach resort has grown to immense proportions, a prototype for some 400 similar spas throughout the country.

But people like Hoff have had the imagination and drive to carry them to their goals. What about those who seem to lack those qualities? Can they also be turned into self-starters? I put this question to Donald Sheff, director of "Mr. Executive," a management development course offered in several cities. I asked him how he goes about trying to turn an ordinary young fellow into a dynamic, strongly motivated self-starter.

"We urge him to study the cases of people like himself who found better ways of doing dull, routine jobs," Sheff said. "We try to make a man understand that there *must* be a better way of doing his job, whatever it is, and that if he wants to stand out among his colleagues he has to find a better way. Once he starts actively seeking it, he has to that degree become a self-starter—and he is on his way up."

Business leaders agree on the importance of encouraging people to put their own ideas into action. They scoff at those who say, "A man either has the inner drive or he hasn't—if he isn't born that way, you can't change him." Several eminent psychiatrists also have told me that strong self-motivation may flare up in a person at any time in his life. [Author's note: Better read that one over again.] All he has to do is find something that he wants so enthusiastically or so desperately that he will give every ounce of his energy and skill to get it.

History is full of cases that confirm this view. Heinrich Steinweg, for instance, was a humble cabinetmaker in his middle years before an idea electrified him and turned him into a hard-driving self-starter. Abandoning all other projects, he brought wood and wire into his kitchen home and built the first Steinway piano.

The head of a medical college told me about a quiet, plodding pharmacist in his 40's who decided one day that he simply had to be a physician; nothing else would fulfil his life. He hired a man to run the pharmacy for his family and went to medical school. He became a doctor in his 48th year. Now, in his 60's, he is a successful and extremely happy physician. "Don't ask me what made him do it," my informant said. "One day he just caught fire. He felt his life would be wasted if he *didn't* do it."

Some people are born with so powerful a sense of self-motivation that they never stop driving themselves. Eighty-year-old pianist Arthur Rubinstein is constantly re-recording compositions that he recorded with great success only a year or two earlier. Once when he told me he was about to re-record some Chopin mazurkas, I said in surprise that I couldn't see why; I thought his previous recordings of these had been perfect. "Nonsense," he said. "Once a man believes that he has achieved perfection, once he loses the motivation to do better, he may as well stop living. He has nothing more to contribute."

This constant urge to do better, to accomplish more, is the priceless asset of the truly self-motivated person. It is one of the things that make him colorful, dramatic, a profitable user of time. When Arthur Brisbane was one of the country's most quoted editorial writers, he returned from lunch one day to find four men playing cards near his office. It was 20 minutes to one. As Brisbane paused, scowling, one of the men nodded at the clock and exclaimed, "We still got 20 minutes before we go back to work. Just killing a little time."

That afternoon Brisbane wrote an editorial that might be the creed of all self-starters. It ended with the words: "The man who is always killing time is killing his own chances in life. The man destined for success *makes time live* by making every minute useful."

The hardest thing I ever did was write a novel. It was as hard as writing this book on salesmenship. There was nobody to tell me to get off my duff and go to work. There were no set hours. I used to wonder why so many authors left their homes to write a book or a play. The reason is distraction! And you'll get it from all sides. Your friends don't want you to succeed. Did you have some crazy idea they did? I told one of my best friends, when he asked me to play golf with him, that I had started to write a book. I wanted to stay with it, as I was getting on pretty well.

"You, write a book?" he replied. Come on, don't be nuts. There aren't many days like this to play golf."

Trying to be a self-starter is not easy.

One time, when I was on the same program with Earl Nightingale, he told the audience the following:

"Ladies and gentlemen, tonight I'm going to tell you how you can make more money than you can spend." (As soon as Earl finished that line I thought, "Tell us now and we'll all go home early.")

"I want all you people to get up an hour early tomorrow morning. If you get up at eight, get up at seven. If you get up at seven, get up at six! Take a pad and pencil and go into the kitchen. Make yourself a pot of coffee. Then I want you to sit down and write down all the ideas you can think of for doing a better job for your company."

There was dull silence, while the audience wondered how an idea like that was going to make them more money than they could spend.

Nightingale continued, "You might not write down one item the first day, but keep in mind as you continue this practice every day that it only takes *one* good idea to change your whole life style." Then Nightingale told the audience about people who have come up with one idea, just one, and struck it rich. He told us about a woman who invented the fastener that is used on overalls. She and her family have been living off that better idea for over 100 years. He told us about the man that thought up the idea of barbed wire. It was the only good idea the man ever had, his family said. He didn't need two; that one did it. Nightingale suggested that you might find a better way to make the product you're selling, or a better way to market it.

91

I went for it. The next morning I was up at six o'clock! I sneaked out into the kitchen with a legal size pad and ball-point pen. I don't drink coffee so I made a pot of tea. I wasn't more than about three minutes into my figuring out how I could do a better job for Fedders Corporation when my wife said, "Who's that in the kitchen?"

"It's me, darling."

A pause, then, "It's six o'clock in the morning! Are you sick?"

Now what the hell was I going to do? Yell back that a guy by the name of Earl Nightingale told me how I could strike it rich?

"I'm not sick," I answered, "I'm making some notes for a meeting."

"Why don't you come back to bed before you wake up the rest of the family and make your notes later?"

I went back to bed. I explained the whole thing the next evening in detail.

As I said, it's tough to be a self-starter. You won't find many friends or even your family patting you on the back and saying, "Right on—you've got the stuff dreams are made of."

I've used Nightingale's simple idea many, many times. Another thing I also know, and have proved, which Earl didn't tell that audience is: "Nothing can stand the assault of sustained thinking" (Voltaire). Then remember a line from the great Goethe's saying: "Only engage, and then the mind grows heated—begin it, and the work will be completed!"

Salvatore Giordano, President and Chairman of the Board of Fedders Corporation, used to assemble the five regional managers, the sales manager and the advertising manager in a room at the Forest Hills Inn in New York to plot the sales and merchandising program for the coming year. We'd start at noon and work until it was time for dinner. Sandwiches were brought up by room service while we continued. Many times we left that room at four in the morning. On one occasion we were ready to break up when the advertising manager said something, I said something and we put it together. It was the germ of an idea that helped us sweep the boards in air conditioning that year. It doesn't seem to make any difference who the idea comes from. I used to use the expression, "The blind pig finally found an acorn."

I don't care who you are, or what your background is, you can come up with a big one. The secret is being a self-starter. You just have to do it yourself. Again, don't ever forget, you won't get too much help and encouragement from your friends and family. They're probably pretty average, and they think it would be kind of nice if you stayed in the same rut with them.

WHAT YOU CAN DO TO SELL YOURSELF RICH:

1. Seize opportunities that others ignore.
2. You must overcome the innate weakness in all of us to be led rather than to lead.
3. When was the last time you put an idea of yours into action? You must have the courage of your convictions.
4. Go against the grain. Don't listen to the negative thinking of the people around you. Find a better way to do something.
5. Some people are born with a powerful sense of self-motivation but it is also something you can develop. But what is hard, in my mind, is that it is so basic, so simple. I once saw a calling card that said on the outside, "How to be a success." You opened up the card and on the inside it said, "GO TO WORK." It's not oversimplification, it's a fact of life. All you have to do is make that simple idea a habit.

Retail Selling

Chapter 19

1. In the following seven chapters the author has selected different kinds of selling and gives tips on how to improve sales in each field:
   a. Retail selling
   b. Distributor selling
   c. The factory representative
   d. Selling securities
   e. Selling gasoline and automotive services
   f. Real estate sales
   g. Selling insurance
2. Among the above you should have no trouble finding examples that will also apply to your profession with a little variation.

I LEAPED ON THIS CHAPTER while I was still hot under the collar. I had just returned from a large local department store. It's something you don't forget easily. There are of course certain things you must do before making a purchase:

1. Have a bloodhound. This is of great help in finding a sales clerk. (I use the word sales clerk very loosely.)

2. When you find one you can only hope he or she will be civil.

3. You will be awe-stricken if you find out he really has a good knowledge of the products in his department.

But you've made the trip and you want to buy. If you're just looking, you're in luck. If you don't bother them, they won't bother you.

On my recent visit I wanted to buy a turtleneck Orlon shirt. When I got to the shirts I found a young string-bean kid standing in front of the cash register talking to two girls behind the counter.

"Pardon me," I said, "I would like to buy a turtleneck. . ."

"Over there," he said and pointed. Over there was a sea of counters with shirts of all kinds. I hunted until I finally found turtlenecks. I could have spent the afternoon hunting for what I wanted, so I grabbed a clerk by the arm and held him.

"My wife bought me this turtleneck I have on," I said. "I want to get another blue one and a white one."

"Have you looked?" he asked me.

"Yes. I can't find any."

"Well, I guess we're out of them."

No offer to show me anything else. No offer to ask if he could order them for me. No turtleneck, period!

Fortune magazine once made the statement, "We could have sold five billion dollars more worth of merchandise last year if we had sales people instead of clerks." And that was said almost ten years ago. Heaven only knows how high the figure is now.

The department stores have the biggest problem, because of their size. And what I'm going to say now might hurt, but the person in charge of each department is the buyer. And Mr. or Mrs. Buyer does not have the right training, in 95 percent of the cases, to train the clerks. The buyer buys and hopes he bought right. If the clerks really knew how to sell, the buyer would be constantly out of inventory!

I talked once to all the people who work for the Hess Brothers department store in Allentown, Pennsylvania. When I finished Mr. Hess insisted that I have a special session for all of his buyers. I asked him why, although I knew.

"You can tell them what I'd like to say. They don't do a good enough job after they've done the buying. I want you to really pour it on." He laughed and said, "No holds barred."

I made that talk for Mr. Hess. He had me back six months later to talk with his people again. He claimed that his sales were up 22 percent, and he attributed a lot of it to the fire and awareness we had built under the clerks and the buyers toward doing a better job.

After I finished with Hess Brothers I got the idea I could spend the rest of my life training and talking to department sales personnel.

I called on the Hecht Company department store in Washington, D. C., first. I bombed out. I remembered what my friend Bill

Hunt always said, "Never talk to a bank clerk, talk to the president." That's what I had done at Hess Brothers, so I also went after the president of Hecht's. He informed me at once that I was in the wrong office. He didn't go over anybody's head. I should be talking to the head of personnel. I did. She was a nice old lady who listened to my story, and then said, "Mr. Hipple, this is April. We don't train people now. Why don't you come back and see us in October."

She reminded me so much of my mother I didn't have the guts to say, "You mean you have a special time for saving people?" A funny thing about that experience was that some years later the Hecht Company department store did have me talk at a year end meeting. Guess who I talked to—all the top executives, not to the image-makers, the ones who were causing all the trouble. They laughed themselves silly at all the cracks I made about bad selling, the lack of training, etc., but that was the problem. Nobody suggested perhaps we should take it a step further and talk to the entire sales force.

How the world has changed. Before World War II Marshall Field and Company in Chicago had the greatest operation in the country. You wouldn't believe how well trained the sales people were, how well they were dressed, the way they looked at you and asked, "May I help you?"

During the war everything went to pieces. You took whatever people you could get so far as help was concerned—and its been going straight downhill ever since.

Now don't get the idea there aren't a lot of good people working for department stores in all departments, but they are completely out-weighed by the ones that appear every day just waiting for payday.

You hear all kinds of experiences from other people. Al Dodge, a master merchandising man for a large distributor, told me of the time he stopped in a store to buy something and a clerk said to him from some distance, "Can I help you?"

"Yes," Dodge yelled, "as soon as you come over here!"

Why all this lethargy? Why don't they *want* to sell all they can? Don't they want any kind of advancement? Wouldn't they like to be an assistant buyer and then a buyer? It's common knowledge that most advancements in department stores come from within.

I gave what I thought was a terrific idea to Hess Brothers department store buyers, an idea of how they could get people to come in free and train their personnel. That really perked their ears up. You see, I know the power the department store has over merchandise salesmen. When the department store whistles, the salesman comes, unless he's a nut. The department store is prestige, it's a showcase. Get your product in there, and you're half way home with the other accounts.

I told the buyers to call up the various companies they do business with, or talk to the salesmen representing these companies. Let's take sporting goods as an example.

The buyer contacts Spalding. He tells them if they want to continue selling to him, send out an expert on tennis rackets, golf clubs, footballs, etc. He wants a man to tell his personnel why Spalding is a better product and what justifies Spalding's price. Sounds like a pretty good idea, doesn't it?

I called Max Hess a month later to see how it was working out. He said, "Worthington, we were really disappointed. We thought that every man they would send out from these companies would be a Hipple. One fellow who comes to my mind was sent from Cannon Mills to talk about linens. He had a movie projector and showed a film of thousands of spindles grinding out bath towels. He was a lousy speaker, and didn't offer any information about how to sell their products."

It's still a good idea, and Max agreed it would work if the companies sent people who knew how to train others—how to multiply manpower.

I guess if I had to pick one thing that stifles selling today it would be attitude. To bring that home to my audiences I always tell the story of young kids today hitching a ride on the highway. Notice it the next time you go for a drive. First, the hitchhiker looks like a slob. Second, he holds his hand down with his thumb out in a manner which says, "Pick me up, the world owes me a living." Remember in the picture, "It Happened One Night," when Clark Gable showed how to hitch a ride! He had that look on his face, meaning he really wanted that ride, and he moved his arm back and forth wiggling his finger begging for the ride. Someone has to get the importance of attitude through to these young people.

There are, of course, thousands of young people making their mark in all facets of industry because they don't think the world owes them a living; but again, too few. The ones who are doing well are exhibiting the right attitude.

Funny that the big shots in the department stores don't realize how much business is walking away every day, because they have too many clerks and not enough trained sales people.

Their biggest problem is that the clerks do not know their merchandise, like the girl whom I asked about the V.I.P. bath towels who didn't even know they were in stock. They know the price only because it's marked on the product. If a woman asks why a pair of gloves costs more than another pair, she won't get an answer.

With the exception of a sale day or during Christmas shopping, clerks have more hours than I want to think about to go over the merchandise in their department and find out why one pair of gloves is worth more. "They're hand-stitched, madam, and they're the finest kid." That's the difference, not just the price.

If you've been wondering why the salesman who sells the buyer doesn't take care of this training, there are a couple of reasons. First, he doesn't fully realize how all that extra night work or early morning work would pay off, and second, he doesn't have the ability in many cases. He doesn't have the ability because he too hasn't been properly trained to multiply manpower.

So it looks like everybody along the line is missing out on the big sell because of too little direction in selling and in how to handle people.

How can the small retail store compete against the giants? He doesn't have the buying power, the advertising or the money, but he does have a little edge.

He may have his share of incompetent people working for him, but he's the buyer and the owner and he's close at hand. He can always leap in and save the day. We won't waste too much time on the fact that the odds are overwhelmingly against him making it big, because he thinks small.

So we must realize that all the billions of dollars worth of merchandise manufactured, sold to distributors and resold to retail outlets—department stores, in particular—move at a pace far below their potential, because of unmotivated, untrained sales people.

WHAT YOU CAN DO TO SELL YOURSELF RICH IF YOU ARE A RETAIL SALES PERSON:

1. You must know all the stock in your department. And you have plenty of time in which to do it. I know, I've been there.
2. Besides knowing your stock you must know it well enough to be able to trade up—sell the <u>difference</u>.
3. Ask the buyer in your department every day if there is some special on sale that you should know about. He'll love you. He will also think about you when it's promotion time. It's not playing up to the boss; it is making an effort to do a better job.
4. Keep all the merchandise in your jurisdiction neat and presentable at all times.
5. If you work in a department store, take some of <u>your own time</u> to study the layout of the store. Where are the other departments?
6. Once more, you are the image-maker. You do all of the things I've stated and more, and you'll find customers asking for you by name. And you'll have those customers telling other people about you, and that is the most powerful advertising in the world. It's called "third party endorsement."

Distributor Salesmen

Chapter 20

RIGHT FROM THE BEGINNING keep in mind that distributor salesmen have no training for their jobs. No degree says they are now equipped to make a life of selling and merchandising. What training they get is from the distributor who might have been a lawyer who made a lot of money and decided to grab a distributorship. He might have been a builder, like one I was involved with. He could be almost anything if he has money. Companies are always looking for someone who has good credit and will buy plenty of their TV and radio sets or whatever distributorship you want to pick.

This man finds himself a sales manager he hires from his competitor, or a son who has had a little experience in selling. We're ready to go.

The manufacturer says he'll take care of the rest. He'll invite the distributor and his salesmen to their regional and national sales conventions. (Note: The distributor very rarely takes the salesmen. It costs too much, he'll tell you.)

Now let's have a look at how the chain of command remains about the same in all selling: the manufacturer, the distributor, the retail outlet.

We've established that the owner or the buyer is the boss in retail selling. He is the man who must inform and train the sales people working for him or under his jurisdiction.

The manufacturer's representative must help train, guide and inform the distributor's salesmen. If he doesn't do a good job, he'll find out that what he has sold the distributor has been merely transferred to another place of storage. If he continues this way, his sales will drop and soon he'll be looking for a new distributor. The last thing he's going to tell his boss is that he failed to do a good job.

The distributor salesman must do the same thing the manufacturer's representative is supposed to do with him. He must now train, guide and work closely with the retail outlet he sold his merchandise to. If he dogs it—we go over the same ground. They have poor sales and pretty soon he tells his boss, "Wilbur's appliance store just doesn't have it. We have to get a new dealer in that territory."

The distributor salesman is given all the tools to do a very successful job for his company and the manufacturers they represent. In most cases he'll be backed by national and local advertising. Spec sheets will be available on all products, as well as a wide variety of point of sale material. He has excellent credit terms to offer his dealer and, last but not least, he generally has a product that the dealer needs. If all this is true, why don't more of them do a better job and make more money?

Most of it is lack of that persistence we talked about earlier; failure to plan his work and work his plan; his constant mistake of just calling on his pet accounts—places where he feels sure he can get an order every time he calls. He hates to break new ground, and new ground is where more business is. Time after time sales managers continually have to keep asking their men, "Why the tight little circle? Why out of 135 accounts do you call on 20 percent of them every week and the other 80 percent only now and then?" Certainly all accounts can't be made into winners, but I have proven as others have that there is a heap of business lying fallow for want of some salesman to do a little plowing.

Gray Matter, an in-house publication of the Gray Advertising Company, published an interesting account of how many times salesmen called on a new account. I don't remember the exact figures, but they were enough to jar the average salesman. A close check showed that salesmen call on new accounts once. If they don't get an order or response, 67 percent of them never go back. The report showed that most of the accounts took a fourth call to make a strike.

I used to tell my salesmen, "What the hell makes you think your customers are a Salvation Army Post? Begging for an order everytime you walk in is a lousy way to get business." I'd tell them to have a *plan* before they went in. Show the dealer you have his interest at heart, genuine interest.

Mr. Distributor Salesman's job is simple. I proved it myself and then turned around and proved it several more times. I've always had a belief I could make a damn good salesman out of a man with little or no experience in selling. The first edge I'd have is that he had no preconceived ideas. Second, he didn't know it couldn't be done. I took one man who had been a carpenter all his life and one who was a clerk in a small-town hardware store. Granted, they both believed in me, which was another big plus in training them.

If you can learn to remember all there is to being a good carpenter, you sure can learn the fundamentals of selling. I know that a good carpenter can't do a bad job. It goes against his grain. He doesn't just hope the corners are straight, he makes them straight. I used that with my carpenter. I told him to do exactly as I told him—not to try and mastermind it, not to listen to any ideas or hints from the other salesmen. That was just a nice way of saying they'll try and drag you down to their level. They'll suggest you don't kill it for them—make too many calls, put up too much advertising material.

To my surprise, my carpenter, selling Fedders air conditioners, Motorola radios and TV's and Bendix washers, had no trouble learning all about the products, and he understood the spec sheets better than any salesman I'd ever met. He had looked at so many blueprints it was all child's play to him. I outlined his territory and told him he was to call on *all accounts*. Then I went over the advertising program and told him what would be expected of him in merchandising the advertising. Then I patiently explained to him that, unlike being a carpenter who could be out of work many times a year due to bad weather, he could work every day, rain or shine, for us. And, last but not least, I told him what his guaranteed salary would be and how much extra I thought he could make on commission over his draw. He made a jackass out of me. In the first six months he made a total of what I figured he could make in a year. The territory was average, maybe a little above. It was beautiful to watch in execution. Like a robot he followed instructions. Like Lombardi said, "You don't do things right some of the time—you do them right all of the time." My ex-carpenter learned the basics, and didn't neglect them.

My sales clerk from the country hardware store also did a wonderful job. I had to be sure he didn't emulate all the salesmen who had been calling on his father's hardware store for so many years. But he, too, didn't have a lot of preconceived ideas, and he was a worker. He topped all my men in the number of calls he made and the amount of advertising he put up. And, last but not least, the dealers used to tell me how Mason would help them move sets around, polish up his, etc. I never had to tell those two men what I often said to some of my other salesmen, "When everything else fails, why don't you start doing what the home office tells you."

WHAT YOU CAN DO TO SELL YOURSELF RICH IF YOU ARE A DISTRIBUTOR SALESMAN:

1. You must be able to give a good presentation to the sales people working for the dealer you sell to.
2. <u>You</u> must see that your dealer always has enough spec sheets and other advertising material to do a first rate job.
3. <u>You</u> must put up all the point of sale material you can. If you just leave it with the dealer, it will never see the light of day.
4. By your actions you must show your dealer that you are not just interested in transferring the place of storage.
5. Don't be a one stop salesman. Keep calling back on that dealer until he has your line. The facts have proven that more sales are made on the fourth to sixth call. Don't give up easily.
6. Be sure and check the dealer's credit before you make a call on him. If he has a poor credit rating, who needs him?
7. Never duck your dealer's sales meeting. It's the beginning of the end if you do.

The Factory Representative

Chapter 21

AFTER THIRTY-FIVE YEARS of experience I've often wondered what most factory representatives would think if they knew what so many of their accounts think of them.

They are the ones who prompted "Whats in a Name" as reported by Dartnell Corporation. "Nearly four in ten companies use ego-puffing titles for salesmen. Among those in vogue: Key account supervisor, executive representative, resident engineer and communications consultant." The ones I've been associated with have been district managers, regional managers and state managers.

Remember, their real job is the multiplication of manpower. If they can't do this, they'll never be able to make quota. They have to see that all those salesmen working for all those distributors are out selling their factory's product every working day. Let's stay with that statement, multiplication of manpower. I learned it in 1940. It was the closest I ever came to losing my job. I was working for Youngstown Kitchens of Warren, Ohio. I was the regional manager for the midwest and had one district manager working for me at the time. Modern steel kitchens were a whole new ball game then. To be more exact, about ten people in the country had what we know of today as a modern kitchen. I had a contract that said I would get 5 percent on all the sales I made in my territory. For your information, a carload of kitchens can run into a nice piece of change, to say nothing of the wall and base cabinets that go with them. All the leads that came into my territory first came to my office. It hurts to be this honest, but here goes. My district manager and I would take the leads and go out and sell the customers ourselves. Then we would go to a dealer, give him the order and sign him up as a dealer. Boy, did the district manager and I work nights! I still don't know how the

105

hell the home office found out what I was doing, but they did. I was called to Warren, Ohio, by the sales manager, Frank Knecht, Jr., and this is what he told me.

"Worthington, you're way ahead of your quota, and I for one think you're a terrific salesman, but understand this. We didn't hire you to sell kitchens. *We hired you to multiply manpower*, and for no other reason."

I got back on the track and never violated that multiplication of manpower theme again. I might add that the president of the company bet me 100 silver dollars (a nice piece of change in 1940) I wouldn't make my quota. He blew the 100 silver dollars, and once more I found out how much you can make selling right. In 1940 I made over thirty-four thousand dollars selling Youngstown Kitchens through distributors and dealers by multiplication of manpower.

The factory representative has it made. He has everything we've mentioned regarding the distributor salesman. He's fortunate enough to have men in the home office with a wealth of background to guide him.

One of the biggest problems he has to guard against is letting his order-taking routine throw him.

We used to have one who called on us four times a year. On those four occasions it was an accepted fact that we were to order for whatever quarter was coming up. I remember one time he got a little upset because we were taking too long to make up our minds about the order. After he got the order we knew from experience we wouldn't see him again for another four months. I would have reported the bastard, because in a sense he worked for us—it was in the price of the product we bought. But I wasn't the president of the distributorship. It's sad to relate that he represented a company that's about 66th in *Fortune's* 500 biggest companies in the United States.

I've never understood why distributors didn't get more factory reps fired—why they covered for them. I had to fire a district manager of mine some years ago. Afterwards, I called all five of the distributors he serviced, or was supposed to, and told them that I was sending up a man I was sure would do a good job for them. Here is what three of the five said: "Anybody you send up will be better than the man we had." From this you might infer I wasn't doing my job. Well, it taught me a good lesson. The man was a liar; his reports were all lies and he drank too much. But I never saw him even take a drink when he was at the factory or when I was with him in the field. And not one dealer or distributor had the brains to tell me he was entitled to have a sober district manager who didn't hate work.

It's the job of every manufacturer's representative to be in the field at all times; that is, if he really wants to know what's happening in the marketplace. If he really wants to help his distributor do a better job, he has to be on the job. He has to forget that nice calling-card the factory gave him, the ego-puffing card that often goes straight to his head.

The factory rep must be out having sales meetings with the salesmen of all his distributors. He has to be able to galvanize other men into action. He has to understand the purpose of the advertising and how it should be merchandised. It is his job to see that his distributor has plenty of point of sale material, and that it is used in the most judicious manner. The material costs his company and his distributor money. If you had the money for all the unused point of sale material in distributors' warehouses you could retire like a king.

When I first started out with Fedders Corporation we were little fish in a big, big pond, with competition such as RCA, Westinghouse, Admiral, Philco, General Electric, etc.

We couldn't afford the luxury of not making every piece of sales material, advertising, the whole lot, work itself to death for us. It was some crew Salvatore Giordano, Sr., surrounded himself with. While all those other fat cats were under the pathetic delusion that they could do it with the name of their company alone, we scuttled them all. Fedders, in a short span of years, became king in the air conditioning business, and still is. And to think that the other companies had millions to spend on advertising against us. But it doesn't mean much if it isn't used, does it?

It all starts with the manufacturer. Failure anyplace along the line is fatal. If the manufacturer's representative does a good job, the odds are the distributor will. And with the distributor doing a good job, the odds are that the retail outlet will be doing a good job.

We'll take a close look at our manufacturer's representative because he's the one that has to funnel all that the manufacturer has to offer down to the right parties.

What's his background and how well is he trained? From fair to bad in both cases. I made a survey of 212 men representing large-manufacturing companies. It's true that 38 percent of them had college degrees of one kind or another, but of this 38 percent, only four had taken business administration as his major.

The usual training at many factories is a trip through the plant, say a couple of hours. The rep now knows how the product is made. He is then shown how to make out his daily report forms, his expense account, etc. The sales manager will, of course, go over his territory and show him his quota for each distributor. If the man being hired has to have technical knowledge, he'll get it.

He's now ready to direct sales as a representative for the company.

What's he lacking? He has little or no knowledge of credit. He knows about advertising from watching his TV set. He is also lacking in the fundamentals of merchandising. About 90 percent of all men in all professions are bad speakers. I don't expect them to be as good as Bill Gove or Cavett Robert, but a manufacturer's rep should be able to talk to small and large audiences and be able to hold their attention. He should be able to deliver his message without reading it word for word. After all, everytime he opens his mouth he and his company are being judged.

I've made every man who ever worked for me take the Dale Carnegie course in public speaking. It's a priceless asset. And I never allowed the company to pick up any of the tab for a salesman. When he puts out his own money, he has a habit of showing up for every session. Of my own success, I would say conservatively that 40 percent to 50 percent of it has been because of my ability to speak. When I got my first job as a district manager for Schenley, my boss, Jake Sabitt, told me that I was to visit all the sub-jobbers, and I was to hold sales meetings with them every week. When I was with Youngstown Kitchens I was told the same thing: hold sales meetings with the distributor salesmen and with the dealers' sales people. It was the same with Ampro Corporation; and by the time I hit Fedders Corporation, I was a pretty good speaker. I must have sounded pretty poor when I made those first talks, but everytime I talked I got a little bit better. You will too.

But the Dale Carnegie course makes you do something you won't do by yourself. You should take it. Your speaking will improve that much faster. It's your greatest insurance, because some day the company might just say, "Harold, we'd like to have you say a few words at the national convention on the improvements on our new line of power tools. You might also mention the expanding market." That's when you die a little, if you've never studied public speaking. It's eight to five you read the whole thing from a piece of paper. You'll be nervous, you'll have no change of pace, and you'll wonder how you got into such a horrible fix.

Now, if you are ready for such an assignment, they'll call on you again, and pretty soon the company will begin to take a second and third look at you. It happened to me at Ampro and Fedders Corporation.

Our factory man should also know something about advertising. He should know so much that not one distributor can take advantage of his company. In too many instances the distributor will usurp the co-op program from the manufacturer. You can never watch the distributor too closely. When newspaper ads are being run in the local market, the manufacturer's representative should be sure the distributor isn't letting the dealers run ads they make up by themselves. Make them use the ad mats. The manufacturer's rep shouldn't allow them to be running ads in papers and on local programs that give the dealer a puffed-up bill. He should see that the distributor has plenty of point of sale material and that it is being used by the salesmen. And on this point he should spot-check himself. He has to understand merchandising. He has to be able to explain it clearly and to galvanize others into action.

Everything we've talked about any person can learn if he has the will and determination to want to do a good job and get ahead.

I can't tell you how many times I've been amused at men sent out by factories to talk to heads of distributing companies. They sent a boy to do a man's job. Here we have a district or regional manager sitting across from the head of a distributorship. The president of the distributorship, in most cases, has been in business for years. He's successful or the manufacturer's rep wouldn't be there. He's smart, and the rep better have the answers when he asks for them. If he decides to go with the manufacturer's line, the same pattern will continue and the representative still better have the answers. I'm sorry to say I've never seen a district manager and I've seen few regional managers capable of dealing with distributor heads. Why? Lack of training.

WHAT YOU CAN DO TO SELL YOURSELF RICH IF YOU ARE A FACTORY REPRESENTATIVE:

1. Your biggest job is <u>multiplication of manpower</u>.
2. You must be an effective speaker—a motivator. If not, it's the Dale Carnegie course all the way.
3. Don't go for the distributor salesman, go <u>with</u> him. You must be effective enough to train each salesman. Do a good job and you won't have to go back, except of course for refresher courses.
4. You, too, must guard against just transferring the place of storage. Once you overload for your own selfish motives, you're in big trouble. You've killed the chance for future orders.
5. In seeking a new distributor be sure you check his credit carefully before you waste your time and the company's. Find out with legwork how the distributor is rated by the dealers. Don't fall into the trap I once did as a young man. I was sure the first distributor I talked to was the answer to a maiden's prayer. Lucky my boss was with me! I also thought the second one we called on was pretty good. The fourth one was the one who got the Schenley distillery line for the state of Wisconsin. He was our distributor for eleven years.
6. If you do a good day's work for your company you won't have to become a fiction writer to fill out your daily and weekly reports.

Selling Securities

Chapter 22

YOUR LOCAL STOCKBROKER, if you have one, goes through a very arduous training course. The biggest emphasis is placed on the rules set down by the Securities and Exchange Commission. Each man or woman must take an SEC exam and pass it. But the exam doesn't place the same emphasis on selling as it does on knowing what a debenture is, how to sell short, etc.

The securities industry has an unusual practice I've never quite understood. In each brokerage office each man has what is called a duty day. The man who gets the duty day also gets all the walk-ins, or people who call on the phone for information about stocks and bonds. It's certainly an excellent way to get prospective customers, some good, some bad.

It has a flaw, as I see it. True, it is my opinion, but I trade a lot of securities each year and have observed this flaw over and over again. Let's assume it is you who walks into a brokerage office on any given day because you're bullish on America. You're a strong personality. The man you get, whose duty day it is, is a much weaker personality. It will never work out. He'll have a tendency to do everything you ask him. Suppose you're a weak individual and the duty day broker is also a weak person. Nothing happens. Suppose you and the broker are both strong personalities. In that case, unless the broker is willing to subjugate himself to you, you too will go no place. What you should do—and about one-half of one percent know this—is walk into the office and make the statement that you are going to invest, but you will make up your mind later as to which broker you wish to entrust your investments with. You must respect your broker and have faith in his judgment; and you won't find much out by a chance meeting with the man who just happens to have the duty day on the day you walk in.

In this engagement period you can find out if your broker really has his hand on the pulse of the market and has a good understanding of your particular needs.

Let me tell you a true story of what happened to me and an associate of mine. We were a broker's dream. We traded securities. And we both expected to have a broker who would work for our interests. Ours was a loser. He was a weak individual—to put it mildly! If we felt we didn't get a good buy order on a stock, he'd never challenge it. He didn't do much homework. About the only thing he was willing to do was write up our orders. It was embarrassing, but both my friend and I finally had to go to the head of the office and tell the manager we were going to stop trading if we couldn't switch brokers. They don't like to do it, but they also don't like to lose two good accounts like ours so they let us change. Well, out of all the brokers in that large office, how did we pick our new broker?

There was a young fellow in that office, much younger than I. My friend and I kept noticing that any time one of the brokers, young or old, didn't know something, he'd yell, "Ed, why is Interstate Department Stores going up?" or "Why has Pan Am gone off three points in two days?" Ed always had the answer. And he always had something in black and white to back it up. What we found out was that he was the first one in the office in the morning, and before the market opened he had thoroughly read *Barrons, The Wall Street Journal*, and the financial page of *The New York Times*, to say nothing of *Business Week* and *Forbes*. He was a mild-mannered chap, but he'd quietly explain offerings that were coming out and stocks that he had studied that had a comeback situation. Here's a good laugh: At one time the office was going to let him go, until my friend and I switched to him. When a new customer would come in, we didn't make any bones about asking them if they had a broker. If they didn't, we'd tell them to get Ed. Here's the punch line: In one year we did such a good job selling him to other people, we could hardly get him on the phone. He's the top broker in that office today.

I have the feeling that too many brokers don't consider themselves salesmen. Most of them have college degrees from good schools and like to think of themselves as "investment counselors."

They don't seem to know you can be an investment counselor but you had also better be a good salesman.

They have an unusual product to sell: It can be bought at any brokerage house in the country for the same price. What do they really have to sell? Their house, its research department and themselves. Oh, how many of them are guilty of being too busy chopping wood to take time to sharpen their axes!

Example: I walked into the offices of one of the largest brokerage houses in the country in San Francisco. I asked a well-groomed young man if I could get a quote on Curtiss-Wright. It was selling at about 11½ to 12 at the time. The broker's answer to me was, "I don't follow that stock." He was nice enough to stroll over to his machine and get me a quote.

After he had given it to me I said, "Do you think because General..."

He cut me off with, "Sir, I don't happen to follow that stock."

Man, did I want to tell that young man what I really thought of his last remark. On the front page of that day's *Wall Street Journal*, at eye level, was a story saying that General Motors had agreed to pay Curtiss-Wright fifty million dollars—yes, $50,000,000—for the rights to the Wankel Engine. And his answer to me was he didn't follow that stock. Boy, was he ever too busy chopping wood!

It was Robert Louis Stevenson who said over a hundred years ago, "Everybody lives by selling something." I wonder if that young broker knows that?

(See Next Page for What You Can Do to Sell Yourself Rich)

**WHAT YOU CAN DO TO SELL YOURSELF RICH
IF YOU SELL SECURITIES:**
1. Before the market opens you should read:
    a. The Wall Street Journal from cover to cover
    b. Barrons
    c. The financial page of The New York Times.
    I won't accept any alibis. All the above are tax deductible for your job.
2. You must also read Business Week or U.S. News and World Report as soon as it hits the newsstand, and Fortune magazine once a month.
3. Think "salesman"! Forget "broker." If you don't, you'll never have any brokerage duties to perform—like writing orders.
4. Have patience! Answer those questions asked you on the phone—even if it kills you! Be utterly charming. If the caller doesn't become a customer, he just might refer you to someone else who will become a customer.
5. If you can't answer a question, admit it. Tell the customer you'll get the answer and be sure you follow through.
6. I can buy your product in hundreds of brokerage houses and at the same price. Sell yourself and your house by the image you create AND THE KNOWLEDGE you offer a customer because you have read the financial publications every day you go to work.
7. You can't beat the odds. Nobody ever has. The more calls you make, the more contacts you make, the more securities you'll sell.

Selling Gasoline and Automotive Services

Chapter 23

HAVE YOU GOT A PROBLEM! Everything you have is something you want to sell, and you may be saddled with the world's worst sales people. You have the drop-outs of America working for you.

How ironic. A company like Exxon, Standard Oil of New Jersey—the second largest corporation in the world—rises or falls on what happens at those gas stations. I'm sorry, I should have said service stations—they corrected me when I talked at many meetings for them all over the country. Now get this shocker: driveway salesmen are responsible for 50 to 90 percent of all contacts with the motoring public! Imagine having that many customers thrown at your face every day of every year. And, to add insult to injury, the motoring public *needs* what the service station has to sell.

You don't drive into a tire salesroom to buy gas, to have a windshield wiper replaced, to change oil or get your car greased. You don't drive into a store that sells automobile batteries to get any of the things mentioned above. You find out in a service station, if they're doing their job, when you need a new battery. You can find out in a service station that your tires are in bad shape.

You could buy your own private jet and a couple of spares if you had the money for all the tire sales and battery sales alone that waltz right out of the average service station. Why? Reasons like specialization, having sales people instead of dummies, inventory, etc.

I've given talks for three of the largest oil companies in the country. They have service stations strewn from one end of the United States to the other. The men who own the service stations are hard workers. Their big problem is that they can't work at the

115

station twenty-four hours a day. One of the biggest laughs I ever got at a sales meeting was when I was talking to over 700 service dealers and their wives in Philadelphia. I had told a couple of jokes that made them laugh and then after a pause I said, "It's nice to have an audience like this, enjoying themselves and laughing so hard, knowing they have left their entire business back home in the hands of those drop-outs!" They roared with laughter.

I talked my head off to those people. They liked what they heard, and knew they could use the information I passed on to them. Sad but true, it all goes back to the same story. What we need is *multiplication of manpower*. If you haven't guessed it, the owner is not equipped by nature or training to go back to his drop-outs and make real sales people out of them. What the oil companies don't do is *invite the drop-outs and leave the owners home*.

When I first started to talk at meetings for Esso, their wonderful advertising program, "Put a Tiger in Your Tank," was at it's height. (For your information that advertising program ranks as one of the all time greats.) I asked the vice president who hired me the following question: "When the service station employee comes out to every car that pulls into the station why doesn't he say, 'May I put a tiger in your tank?'"

The vice president paused for a moment and said, "Mr. Hipple, if you can find a way to get them to do it, we'll write you a check for $50,000, no questions asked."

Seems rather simple, doesn't it? And it would work, if they did it. You ask enough people that question, "May I put a tiger in your tank?" and a big percentage, without thinking, are going to say yes. It's only after they're driving out that they'll think to themselves, "Holy Moses, I put premium gas in my car."

You get a real curve thrown at you when you watch the service station commercials on national television. It's raining and cold out and a good-looking man comes charging out to your car with a smile the toothpaste people would love. But what really happens? A kid who looks like he's rolled in the grease pit comes out minus the smile, with hair down to his shoulders, and some clothes on he got from Good Will. *He cannot—* I repeat, cannot— find out how to get the hood up to check your oil or the battery. If the owner is also on duty, you're safe. He runs to the boy's rescue.

You have most likely had your own personal experiences at your local service station. Here are some gems from my experience.

I drive in and tell the young man to fill it up. While he is in the process of doing this, three other kids about his age walk over and grab hold of the back bumper of a two-door Vega, lift it up and turn the car all the way around. The kid waiting on me with his hair blowing over his shoulder in the breeze has a big grin on his face as he watches. There are two very cute teenage girls sitting in that Vega. During all the laughter, fun and games the gas is overflowing from the pump and shooting all over my car. The owner is not there, so he has no idea of how his drop-out is cementing relations with the customers.

On another occasion, after I had purchased some gas, the kid took my money with no effort to clean my windshield. I asked him if he would. He did, and walked away again. Granted my Jeep is four years old, but it only has 22,000 miles on it. I called him back again and asked why he hadn't checked my oil. He looked at me, then the Jeep, and said, "I didn't think you cared about the oil in this car." If I had more time I would have gotten out of the Jeep and said to the kid very patiently, "Son, did it ever occur to you that this Jeep might need the oil checked *more* than a new car?"

Sometimes you can be fooled by good service. It happened to me. I was in the Jeep again, and after my car had been filled with gas, one kid was cleaning the front windshield, one was checking the oil and the payoff was, one was cleaning my back window. A few seconds later I got the answer. A truck pulled away from in front of the service station window and there was a big sign, UNDER NEW MANAGEMENT! They'll shower you with attention as a new customer. In about two months they'll let you pump the gas yourself and the only service you'll get is the service you ask for. They never seem to realize that it's fine to get a new customer, but it's bad to lose the old one. Trading old ones for new ones is poor business. Sure, I've gotten a lot of good service from the drop-outs when the boss was watching. My trouble is I don't catch the owner in enough times.

There are countless minutes rolled into hours during the day when the employees could be finding out the facts about the various batteries for sale, tires, etc. After a close study (so I'd have the facts when I talked to the owners of the oil companies) I found most of the spare time was spent drinking Cokes, working on some wheels they had parked on the service station lot, talking with other kids who dropped by and talking on the phone to their girls.

Apparently the service station owner has a hard time finding help. If he gets too rough, the kid will quit. The boy doesn't take any back talk from his parents, and he's not about to take too much from the boss. He can always get a job at another service station.

If the owner could control his help, he'd make it a point to go over the tires, batteries and accessories (TBA, as the service stations refer to them) every morning as religiously as he opens the pumps.

I've been at oil companies' sales meetings where the owners have been told how to go about checking tire wear and battery wear on a customer's car. How they've been told not to ask if they can check the oil, but to check it! How they should suggest a can of de-icer for the windshield with winter coming up. Maybe I'm in a class by myself, but they sure don't try any of those above-mentioned sales talks or services on me.

How can you sell tires and batteries if you don't display them? The oil companies have to put on a real effort to get the owner to buy this kind of equipment. If the service stations were doing the kind of job they should be doing, the tire and battery stores would lose half their business. Again, the logical place for the sale to take place is in the service station. The oil companies have good tires, batteries and accessories. They have as good a price, but they die on salesmenship and inadequate inventory most of the time.

So, as usual we're back to square 1 because of the lack of selling and training. Everything else is there. As I said in the beginning, the service station is backed by powerful advertising and merchandising and all the right equipment to make our cars perform, from a grease job to a set of new tires. The owner can get everything he needs with a telephone call—advertising, inventory of all kinds. It's all so easy—easy, until the owner has to hire additional help. Let me quote Webb Lowe, President of Bonanza Steak Houses: "Our biggest problem is human resources—attracting, hiring, training, developing and promoting human resources."

So if it's Mr. Lowe's biggest problem, you can well understand the problem facing the owner of a new service station—a man who probably has little or no management training, no selling experience.

WHAT YOU CAN DO TO SELL YOURSELF RICH IF YOU ARE IN GASOLINE AND AUTOMOTIVE SERVICES:

1. The owner must discipline himself to follow the rules set down by the company—all of them.
2. Employees must not be allowed to park their heaps on the service station property.
3. Employees must wear the company uniform at all times, must be clean and must look neat.
4. Every free minute, the owner must constantly keep <u>training the employees</u>: how to open the hoods of all cars; to offer to help customers put air in their tires instead of standing around and watching the customer in action; to know the prices of all products—above all, the merits of products he can sell by trading up the customer.
5. If the owner will see to the above and give top priority to the multiplication of manpower, then—and only then—can he increase his earnings.

Chapter 24

Real Estate Sales

TO SELL A PIECE OF COMMERCIAL PROPERTY, a house, a commercial building, or rent an apartment, in most communities you must have a real estate brokers license. This is not easy to obtain. You have to prepare for it, take an examination and above all, pass. If you do you'll know all about deeds, contracts, etc., but you still won't know a damn thing about salesmanship. It doesn't come with the brokers license. This you will learn from the personnel of the company you're going to represent. How well they are equipped to train you is debatable. That is not said in rancor or bitterness. It is said after dealing with real estate sales representatives for over thirty years. I have bought houses, apartment buildings, commercial land, commercial buildings, land and rented apartments.

How about the background of some of our real estate sales people? Some have been lieutenant colonels in the Army, captains in the Navy, retired bookkeepers or any person who simply thought selling real estate might be his cup of tea. Most of them don't know it's a profession that calls for being a self-starter.

I have run into two good real estate sales people—both women.

I don't know what they tell their sales people at the home office. What I do know is, they haven't taught them that they have a duty to do the best they can for their customers. Example:

In 1958 I was told that the old Methodist Church in Vienna, Virginia, was for sale. They had built a new one. While you're chuckling, keep in mind a church is built on land, and besides the land the building has some merit. I looked it over and saw that I could take the steeple off, do a little other remodeling and turn it into a commercial store. I contacted the real estate broker. The asking price for the land and the building was $12,500, an absolute steal at that price. While I was walking down the block with the real estate broker to go into the building, he said to me: "I think you can get it for $8,000."

I liked what I heard, but I thought about how the church people would love the great selling job the broker was doing. I eventually got it for $8,500.

Some years earlier I bought Hunter Mill Farm in Oakton, Virginia. The broker (the worst I ever dealt with) told me the property was for sale for $47,500, another helluva good buy. After three visits to the farm I finally met the owner, and you can imagine my surprise when I found out he thought I was being quoted *his* price of $53,000. I finally got it for $49,000. I give you my word I would have paid the owner's asking price. I wanted that farm.

In 1961 I bought the May Rug Company, the land and building, from the owner. He quoted me a price, and try as I would I couldn't budge him. I even offered all cash—no sale. I finally paid his price.

Who do you suppose tells all those real estate brokers to whack five, ten or twenty thousand off the price *for openers*? I still haven't found out.

A couple of years later I was interested in buying a large lot in the center of Vienna, Virginia from Safeway Stores. The broker told me they were asking $2 a square foot and in his next breath said, "Offer them $1.50 a square foot."

I could tell you of a lot more personal transactions, but I'm sure I've made the point. The broker not only screws himself out of commission, but CHEATS the customer he or she is representing.

I recently talked to the head of one of the largest real estate houses in the Washington, D. C., area. He said the rate of attrition is frightening. The reason for the fast turnover is as old as time: "You can't make a silk purse out of a sow's ear." You can't make a good real estate broker out of just *any* retired or bored person or someone who thinks they'd like to give it a fling.

You want to buy a house. How much do you want to know about it? A lot more than you'll get from your broker. You can read, so why doesn't the broker just give you the card he takes from the file and let you do a sort of a "do-it-yourself" buying job? When I think of the times I've asked one of the simplest questions, "How much are the taxes?" and gotten the answer, "Oh, gee, I don't have that with me."

I've checked time and again to see how much homework the broker really does. And the answer is, not enough to represent you or me.

Real estate is a great profession—what a wonderful product to sell! I can still hear my father telling an audience of people who had come down to his company's real estate offices to buy a lot back in the Twenties, the following: "Folks, remember no matter where you go or what you do in this life you either own or rent a piece of real estate." Boy, how he used to read that line. He also used to tell them there was only one thing they could be sure of, "More people and less land."

The rewards can be tremendous for sales persons who are willing to take the time to learn to *sell* instead of *show*.

Remember, a good job done with every prospect earns you the greatest advertising in the world, "third party endorsement."

WHAT YOU CAN DO TO SELL YOURSELF RICH IF YOU SELL REAL ESTATE:

1. Do your homework on any piece of real estate you're showing in an effort to sell. Ask yourself: Do you have all the facts at hand? Do you know what the taxes are, where the schools are, how old the house is, what kind of financing can be had, what condition the appliances, heating and air conditioning plant are in?
2. Have you taken the time to find out something special about the house, building or land that might make it more attractive to your prospective customer?
3. Have you made an effort to find out something about your customer? Does he want it for investment, to live in, etc.?
4. And have you kept uppermost in your mind, Don't forget the A.B.C.'s: "Always Be Closing!"

Selling Insurance

Chapter 25

YOU COULDN'T HAVE PICKED a better field of work. If I had to do it all over again it's the one I'd choose. The idea of being able to help people like you and me and make a lot of money at the same time has a lot of appeal.

It was a long time before I realized how slow on the uptake most of us are. I always wondered why we had to have people to sell life and casualty insurance. It is an absolutely *indispensable product*. Without it you're a river boat gambler.

Selling insurance has changed like everything else. The sales people don't dig as hard as they used to. For example, when I was young the salesmen used to come knocking on my door. Today I receive a piece of mail asking me to tell the insurance company when I was born and they in turn will send me a little notebook with my name printed on it. The best way of course is face-to-face contact. If there is the slightest doubt in your mind do yourself one wonderful favor. Get a book entitled *The Feldman Method*, by Andrew H. Thomson (Lynbrook, N.Y.: Farnsworth Publishing Company). It has to be one of the best and most informative books ever written for anyone who would like to succeed in life. Mr. Feldman is the world's greatest insurance salesman. What you can learn from him is worth the price of the book alone. You get the chance to pick the brains of a man who is pure genius in his field. One more word on *The Feldman Method:* What Ben Feldman does can be applied to *any kind of selling, anyplace, anytime.*

Insurance companies get an "A" for their training of the men they send out into the field, but they, like all other companies, have to live with the element of human failure. And it abounds and abounds.

About thirteen years ago I called up the second or third largest insurance company in the country. I told the salesman that I had been told by my auditor that my wife was going to get a crushing tax bill when I died. He made an appointment, I passed the medical and he sold me a $26,000 policy taken out by my wife that would cover my estate taxes if and when I died. (And as Mr. Feldman puts it, I'm gonna' die just like you and everybody else.) The premium is one thousand dollars a year. It could have been so much less if a good prospecting insurance salesman had caught me about ten years sooner. Now the point of this little story is that I have not heard from the man that sold me that policy in thirteen years. He could have died. I thought of that, so I checked. He's still alive. I know that everybody would be happy to have made as much as I've made since my salesman handed me my little black metal box to keep my policy in and wished me a long life.

I've always wondered why after young couples get married and have a child they don't do the same thing with the newborn baby as they do with their car. As soon as they name the baby they should grab the phone and take out insurance so the child can go to college. Feldman has a neat way of putting it. He asks the parents if they would rather pay the child's college education in four years or in eighteen years. You don't have to be too bright to make that choice do you? Can you imagine the parent driving the car around without insurance?

As I've already said, insurance is one of the great fields to enter both for the satisfaction of helping others and making a very good livelihood. So I close by once more telling you, buy and read *The Feldman Method*. I should really get a finder's fee for bringing you the helpful information in Andrew H. Thomson's book. I found it by chance, you might never have had the same luck.

WHAT YOU CAN DO TO SELL YOURSELF RICH
IF YOU SELL INSURANCE:

1. Don't rely on direct mail. Make calls and knock on people's doors. Face-to-face contact is still the best way to sell.
2. Follow-up on people you have sold to. As their life situations change, they may need additional insurance.
3. Read **THE FELDMAN METHOD** by Andrew H. Thomson.

Stop Conforming!

Chapter 26

1. You have to break out of the mold.
2. What all great men have in common.
3. What Wilfred A. Peterson has to say about "The Art of Changing Yourself."

IT WON'T BE EASY. You've been doing it all your life. From the day you were born you've had the "X" on you. Unhappily you're a product of your home. There's no need to be hung up about it. It's been going on generation after generation, and the young couples having children this very day will be putting the "X" on their children just as your parents did on you.

Your parents tell you, "Don't do this and don't do that." Your friends' parents are telling your friends the same thing. The years keep ticking away and your parents' work is coming into full bloom. In high school you'd rather throw yourself under the school bus than not have the right shoes, the right "T" shirt, the right hairstyle, etc. You have started to feel comfortable at this tender age in the rut most of us will wallow in the rest of our lives. You are emulating the people around you. You are conforming! You are doomed to mediocrity if you keep it up.

It's hard to break the mold. You continue on with the same pattern in college. You graduate and damned if you aren't still on the same kick. Wide ties, bell-bottom pants, long sideburns, John Wilkes Booth mustache. It just might be that *you* look like a jerk with long sideburns. Your face isn't right for a "Booth" mustache. But you no longer have the courage of your own convictions. You lost it years ago following the crowd. I remember a man who was head of the Chicago vice squad telling me once, "If you are trying to escape and your tendency is to run to the right, run to the left and you'll get away."

I was amazed one day to read an article in *Parade* magazine. It went on at great length to tell how all the great men—ALL—had one thing in common: they were *non-conformists*. Remember that saying, "Unusual action creates unusual results."

If you must emulate someone, pick a *successful* person. Has it ever struck you how we all have a tendency to sink to the lowest common denominator—to follow the crowd. It's cozy, being lost in the crowd.

The successful salesmen can take direction and follow it. The average ones are always trying to cut corners, find an easy way out. They keep conforming.

So stop playing "follow-the-conformer" or you'll always be average. You'll never be part of that top 5 percent we mentioned earlier in this book.

It is not too late to change. Tomorrow morning put all your conforming behind you. Listen to what Wilfred A. Peterson has to say about "The Art of Changing Yourself" in *The Art of Living* (New York: Simon & Schuster, 1961):

> MAN ALONE, of all the creatures on earth, can change his own pattern. Man alone is the architect of his own destiny.
>
> WILLIAM JAMES declared that the greatest revolution in his generation was the discovery that human beings, by changing the inner attitudes of their minds, can change the outer aspects of their lives.
>
> HISTORY AND LITERATURE are full of examples of the miracle of inner change. Do you know the Persian story of the hunchback prince who became straight and tall by standing each day before a statue of himself made straight?
>
> CHANGE requires the substituting of new habits for old. You mold your character and future by your thoughts and acts.
>
> CHANGE can be advanced by associating with men with whom you can walk among the stars.
>
> CHANGE can be inspired by selecting your own spiritual ancestors from among the great of all ages. You can practice the kindliness of Lincoln, the devotion of Schweitzer, the vision of Franklin.

CHANGE can be achieved by changing the environment. Let go of lower things and reach for higher. Surround yourself with the best in books, music and art.

After you've read the above, please take it very seriously and don't get the idea that because you're a salesman, you can't cover yourself with a cloak of higher ideals and higher education. The ones who don't want to follow what Wilfred A. Peterson has to say about "The Art of Changing Yourself" *ARE CONFORMING!*

WHAT YOU CAN DO TO SELL YOURSELF RICH:

1. If you're making the same amount of calls your fellow salesmen are, you're conforming.
2. If you put up the same amount of advertising material they do, you're conforming.
3. If you sit at the sales conferences and national conventions listening but not taking notes, you're conforming.
4. If your boss asks, "Are there any questions?" and like the rest you're thinking, "I don't want to rock the boat; I don't want the rest to laugh at my question," you're conforming.

The Big Sell

Chapter 27

1. Everything you learn, everything you use that makes you a better sales person is yours and yours alone. It is an asset nobody can take away from you.
2. Would you make more selling what people need or what people want?
3. Why people buy, and how you should handle it.
4. Do you know how to make a shopper into a buyer?
5. How to use the three buying decisions, Need, Time, and Price.

THIS IS A TALK I GAVE TO the Hess Brothers department store employees when Mr. Hess invited me back a second time to talk to them. I think it will interest you, no matter what you're selling.

You sales people are the most important people in this country. As Jack Lacy says, "Only half of the economy is bought—the other half is sold." You sales people turn the wheels of industry. Whether the raw material producers' business continues to increase depends on how much you sell.

While I'm talking to you I want you to constantly keep in mind that you are two different people. First, you're a sales person; and second, every single one of you is also a buyer. So what we're going to talk about will not only apply to you as sales people but also as buyers.

We're going to talk about fundamentals, psychological facts about people. The points we are going to cover have all been worked out in advance by people skilled in selling techniques.

They'll work for you just as they have for thousands of others if you'll apply them; convert them into a habit, if you will. A good habit is, as William James says, "A technique for simplifying your existence; for saving time and the energy of making decisions."

Keep in mind that everything you learn, everything you use that makes you a better sales person, is yours and yours alone. It's an asset no one can take away from you.

Why do people buy? That may sound stupid on the face of it, but a lot of brilliant people in this country have spent an untold amount of time and money to find out the answer to that simple question—WHY DO PEOPLE BUY? What makes people buy? What is it about any given product that will make people buy more of it? Just recently a new company in New York City opened its doors for business. It is called Motivation Inc. Already many new companies are using their services.

I have in my hand here a pack of Marlboro cigarettes. Not so long ago this cigarette just wasn't selling at all. The company went to Motivation Inc. for the answer. After a study, Motivation Inc. told them a very simple thing—so simple on the face of it, it almost sounds silly. They told Marlboro their packaging was too feminine. Men smoke most of the cigarettes. Gear your packaging to them. And that, ladies and gentlemen, is how we got the package you see me holding. That's how we got a crew-cut man with a face like granite and a tattoo on his fist. They changed their ad to "You've got a lot to like in a Marlboro, filter, flavor, flip-top box." It worked; their sales leaped 22 percent in the first six months of the new packaging and new advertising approach.

Let's face a fundamental truth. It is said that 80 to 90 percent of all the money that is spent is spent for things people want—not things people need. Please get that distinction! People buy those things that they want, not necessarily those things they need. Here's the secret on that subject. Most people honestly believe that they *need* those things that they buy. I'm no different than the rest of you. I'm a buyer, too. I need a Lincoln Continental like I need a hole in my head, but boy, how I want one. If a good salesman got hold of me and appealed to my wants, I would soon convince myself that I *need* a Lincoln.

I'll tell you what you can do to make me happy. You give me the sales from everything the people buy in your store that they want, and I'll give you all the sales from the merchandise they buy that they really need. If you do, I'll beat your sales record by fifty-to-one.

What makes us want? A lot of reasons. Some people buy because they are greedy. Some because they are like pack rats; they just want to acquire. One of the bigger motives is VANITY. And don't get the idea that only you ladies in the audience are vain. Let's take an item like cosmetics, a multi-million dollar market. Why do women buy cosmetics? I asked my wife once, when she came home with sixty dollars' worth of what a lot of husbands would call junk. I challenged my wife for buying creams, powders and lotions. She gave me a very simple answer. She said it made her feel better. Well, if she didn't know, she was buying it to make her more youthful, more beautiful. That's all right with me, and I think it would be all right with any other husband if he can afford it.

Another buying motive: KEEPING UP WITH THE JONESES. One of the finest motivations for a new washing machine, a new TV, a new power lawn mower, is to have something the neighbors can see or hear about. Oh, it's a form of vanity, something most of us would be hard pressed to admit.

The single greatest buying motive, they tell us, is FEAR. More money is spent for this reason than any other. Think of some of the ads you see and read laced with the fear concept. Remember the famous Lifebuoy commercial? "Buy Lifebuoy, you may have B.O." In other words, if you don't buy it, you may smell. It worked; people bought it in droves.

You haven't forgotten "Ipana" so soon, have you? "Watch the danger line." If you don't use their toothpaste your teeth are going to fall out! And they, too, sold thousands and thousands of tubes on that theme.

How many of you people in the audience have insurance? Silly question. I'd answer that question by saying about 99 percent. Why? Why do you have life insurance, health insurance, burglar insurance, fire insurance, automobile insurance, etc? Because you, like me, are afraid. We're afraid we might drop dead or get hit by a truck and the rest of the family will starve to death after we're gone. Or we might have an automobile accident and someone will sue us for all we've got. We're afraid our house might burn down. We're afraid, afraid, afraid. As a result we spend hundreds, yes, thousands of dollars for that protection based on the fear concept. The insurance business is a billion-dollar industry. There is nothing wrong with their approach. We can't afford to be without it. In fact, it's a good thing they do use the fear approach; if not, too many of us would be without it.

I'll tell you how we sold the first refrigerators. Fear. We told Mrs. Housewife who was getting along rather well with her ice-box the following, "You could have bacteria mold; the children could be wiped out." Really? And that was the night she told her husband Charlie, "We have to buy a refrigerator. We're lucky we're not all dead." Nobody took the time to remind that housewife that her Uncle Otto slipped away at ninety-three, and he didn't even have an ice box—kept his food in a smokehouse.

I remember my father telling me about the methods used to sell National Cash Registers over forty years ago: saying to a storekeeper, "Do you realize how much your clerks are stealing from you with that drawer you use to make change?"

One of the men after a sales meeting said to my father, "Mr. Hipple, is that kind of approach quite fair?"

My father said to him,

"John, you do what I've told you and it will be the best unfair trick you ever played on a storekeeper." I found out he was right. It was the best thing that ever happened to the storekeeper—not only did it stop the pilferage of money, it offered a better way of handling his business.

From what I've said, I don't want you to get the idea you should size up each customer and think, "She looks vain," or "He looks like the type who might be afraid," or "I wonder if she is trying to keep up with the Joneses." It's the last approach I want you to take. To be a good sales person you must avoid a big pitfall. It's what I call trying to be the boy with the x-ray mind. *Do not* try and figure out what the customer wants by guessing. It just doesn't work. The pure way, the safe way, is to tell each customer all you know about the product you're selling. Never leave out the smallest detail. When you've been selling long enough, you'll learn that the one you left out might have made the sale.

When I was working for Youngstown Kitchens we brought out a new 66" double bowl sink and undercabinet. It had the following features:

1. Swing type faucet
2. Concealed bread board

3. Six cubic feet of storage space
4. Acid resisting sink top
5. Quiet drawers on brass runners
6. Spray faucet and rubber basket to place dishes
7. Sectioned cutlery drawer
8. Twin bowls both with crumb cup strainers.

You would not believe how many times I would watch some half-baked sales person selling one of our sinks. He didn't mention the acid resisting sink top. He didn't show the bread board. We had some trouble once with some of the sliding bread boards splitting. I went out in the field to check a lot of them. One lady said to me, "What bread board?"

"The one in your sink," I told her. I wish you could have seen her face when I pulled it out. She said she had had the sink for almost a year and didn't know it was there. Maybe the sales person doesn't think the swing-away type faucet isn't a point worth mentioning. I had a lady buy one for almost that very reason. She said she kept hitting her fine china against the stationary faucets.

Sales people have a tendency to think in their money frame. I find this very true in department stores. The clerk may make much less than the customer. She has a hard time showing the more expensive items. I had a girl this last Christmas say to me:

"Oh, you wouldn't want this bath oil. It's twenty-five dollars for only two ounces." It was Royal Secret bath perfume by Germaine Monteil. It was exactly what I wanted. It's the reason I was in the store. They were the only ones that handled that particular brand.

It doesn't make any difference *what the product is*. You tell the prospect everything. And if you do, you'll have that comforting feeling of knowing you've got the edge on your competition.

Let's go to an automobile sales room as we probe deeper into the why of selling. A man we are going to talk about sells Fords. He is a good salesman and knows his product inside and out. Let's assume he has three prospects in the morning. One is a doctor, sixty-two years old. The second one is a young man in his thirties, a bank teller. He doesn't make a lot of money, but he has a job which he feels has dignity. Our third prospect is a twenty-one-year-old fellow in his third year of college. You can't sell them all the same way as they all have different hidden buying motives.

You're going to tell the doctor about the width of the door, how easy it is to get in and out because it rides on ball-bearing hinges. He gets in and out of the car a lot of times. You'd want to point out the heavy-duty battery that will start the car instantly under any weather conditions, another must for the doctor. You'll tell him about the ease of driving and parking with the power steering. You'll tell him everything, with stress on the particular things that would appeal to a sixty-two-year-old doctor.

How about our bank teller? You'll tell him a lot of the same things you told the doctor. He wants a car that says he's a solid citizen, not gaudy or flashy; something that will fit in with his idea of what a banker should purchase. You'll talk to him about the fine re-sale value of the Ford, the excellent service he'll get and show him the color chart of the available rich-looking cars in the Ford line at a fair value in price.

Now for our third prospect. Would you tell him about the wide, easy opening door and the battery as fast as you would the doctor? I don't think so. What is most likely closer to his heart? The engine power, how long will it take him to go from 0 to 60 m.p.h. He wants to feel he'll turn many a pretty girl's head when he drives by. He wants color, straight stick, and all the ginger that he can get.

All these types of buying motives can be translated and moved into the products you sell. But once more be sure you tell the whole story. You might run into a crazy doctor who wants everything the twenty-one-year-old college lad does.

Here is another way to make your sales climb. There are a multitude of buying decisions, but we're going to zero in on the three biggest buying decisions. They are the ones you should know the best and use the most. Everybody must make these three decisions before they buy. They must make a "NEED" decision. They must make up their minds they need this item. They must make a "TIME" decision. They must make up their minds to buy the item today, tomorrow, next week or next year. They must make a "PRICE" decision. They must make up their minds that this particular item is worth the money you're asking for it. When these three decisions are made your prospect will buy. It's your job to ferret them out. It's easy to do, some of them are even automatic.

Suppose a woman walks into your dress department, and with just a few seconds of conversation you find out that she is going to a party—a big party, and she needs a formal gown. A few more seconds of conversation and you find out she needs it Friday, just three days away. We now know she needs a gown and she needs it quickly. Two of the most important buying decisions have been made. The only thing left is for you to show her the right gown at the right price. Yes, I know you can still lose the sale if you don't have just what she wants. But you'll know she didn't walk out because you failed in your job if you show her everything and keep in mind she let you know almost at once that she was two-thirds sold when she walked in because of the need and time factors.

Another lady may walk into the same department. She doesn't need a dress now, but with some conversation you find out she's the banker's wife or her husband is president of the biggest factory in town. So price isn't the most important factor in her buying motive at this time. If you can show her an interesting, exciting dress, she'll buy. Your advantage is that you can show her the best designs because price isn't a factor.

If a man runs into a tire store and says, "I need a tire. I just had a blowout and we're leaving on our vacation tomorrow," the TIME is now and the NEED is now! Show him that you can give him service and value and you have a sale.

You're talking to a woman who walked into your appliance department to look at automatic washers and you ask her if she has ever used one and she says, "Yes I have." The desire is there and with a little more conversation she tells you that hers is nine years old and is no longer repairable. You don't have to spend time convincing her she should buy today, that the TIME is now. The clothes are piling up at home. All you have to do is show her that your automatic washer is the finest buy on the market. It will do the job and at the right price.

I'm not suggesting all this is as easy as falling off of the proverbial log. Good selling is an art like anything else. I've been listening to sales people talk to customers for a long time and you'd be amazed how many times the customer has laid the sale right in the sales clerk's lap before she could say a word.

I watched a lady at a cosmetic counter walk up and say, "I've been using Carter lipstick and I don't like the shade. It's wrong for me." Let's not waste time trying to re-sell Carter. She's already told you what she thinks of it. And it's all bad. Show her something new and flatter her vanity. Remember if Carter was the only lipstick you sold she wouldn't have come in.

As soon as an insurance salesman finds out that the Walkers have had a new son, that salesman has a leg up. What the Walkers might not do for themselves, they'll do for their new son. Now the salesman can talk about how his insurance company can insure that their new son will be able to go to college. The NEED is there. It's the best TIME for the Walkers to buy, and the price is as cheap as it will ever get at the son's age.

We move on to another factor in making more sales. Too many sales people make one sale and lose the next two, and for the life of them they couldn't tell you why. Their answer to the boss or the buyer is that the person was a SHOPPER. Don't ever forget it's our job to make a shopper into a buyer. You first make a statement or a proof of a statement of your product, a statement that is true and sincere. Next you offer proof that the statement you have just made is true. Third, you ask for a commitment. It is vital that the proof you offer should be as dramatic as possible and should leave no doubt in the prospect's mind that your proof is accurate and conclusive. An example: You're in the record department, and the salesgirl tells you the record is unbreakable. She wants to offer proof. She drops it on the floor and proves it.

If you're telling a customer that your material won't shrink, then have a sample of a piece that has been washed, hasn't shrunk and hasn't faded. Your biggest hurdle is asking for the commitment. It's one of the hardest things for sales people to learn and execute. The more you ask for a commitment, the easier it gets. Keep in mind the worst the customer can say is, "I'll think about it," or "I'll come back later," or she'll just walk away. Learn from your mistakes. When you lose a customer you've been trying to sell, for heaven's sake, review everything you said. That's how I found out how to lecture, by my mistakes. It's also how I found out when I was on the right track.

Take what you can from this chapter. But stop standing around waiting for the customers to accost you. Think about these buying motives we've talked about. They work. They've been tried and true for longer than most of you have been alive. You've done it your way; give these new concepts a good try and your sales will increase.

If you want a good lesson on the validity of this chapter and you are going to stay in sales do yourself a favor. Call up a storm window company, call National Cash Register or IBM and pretend you want to buy some of their equipment. You'll get the whole treatment we talked about in this chapter. They'll go through the TIME, NEED, and PRICE bit so fast it will make your head swim and I'll bet you they'll ask for the commitment all day long until they get a straight yes or no answer from you.

WHAT YOU CAN DO TO SELL YOURSELF RICH:

1. You must completely understand the reasons why people buy. Some of the main ones are:
   a. Vanity
   b. Keeping up with the Joneses
   c. Fear.
2. You must always tell the whole story of the product you are selling—not part of it part of the time. What you think is the most saleable point might not appeal to the customer. What you've dismissed as not too important might be just the thing the customer is looking for. I've seen it happen many times.
3. You must know and understand fully the three most important buying decisions. You don't have time to think about it when the customer is in front of you. It must be second nature. They are:
   a. Need
   b. Time
   c. Price.
4. Review every sale you ever attempt to make.
   a. If they bought: Why? What did you say?
   b. If they didn't buy: Why? And don't use the old bromide, they were just shopping. Your job is to make a shopper into a buyer.

   If you spend enough time on a. and b. you'll soon find out the pluses and minuses in your sales presentation.

Sell Yourself Rich

Chapter 28

1. How to give a good sales talk.
2. There are many prime examples of good sales material you can use the next time you address a sales group for your company.

NOW I WANT YOU TO READ the first talk I recorded, titled "Sell Yourself Rich." And in the next chapter we'll go through the second recording I made for the Chicago Businessmen's Record Club, "Hammer Home the Difference." Both talks are filled with ideas to help you sell.

THE INTRODUCTION:

Ladies and gentlemen, at this time the Businessmen's Record Club is proud to introduce you to a talk given by Mr. Hipple to 2,800 people at a Fort Lauderdale Sales Executive rally. Here is Mr. G. Worthington Hipple:

They tell the story about the young man who used to go up to the Concord Hotel in the Catskills every weekend. Every weekend he went up there, he got pinched for speeding. He got pinched going up and coming back. This went on week in and week out. Finally the young man got to know the cop pretty well, there was a kind of esprit de corps between the two of them. The cops name was McGarrity. He kept giving the tickets to the young man who took them and filed them in his glove compartment.

After some time had gone by, the young man was notified that he had inherited a fantastic amount of money. The first thing

141

he thought about when he was told about the money was Officer McGarrity. As soon as he got the money, he went out and bought himself a 300SL Mercedes Benz. (If you ladies don't know, it's a car that will do 160 miles an hour on the flat.)

And the young man started for the Concord Hotel. He stopped first to get a cap. You understand you can't drive one of those cars without one. He was going along 70 miles an hour through a 30-mile zone looking for McGarrity. And pretty soon McGarrity saw him and went out after him. He was right behind the young man yelling, "Pull over," and the young fellow pushed the gas pedal down. He was going about 105 miles an hour. Then he slowed down a little to tease McGarrity. At 90 miles an hour McGarrity was behind him yelling, "Pull over or I'll shoot!" And with that the young man pushed the gas all the way to the floor and shot out and up to 150 miles an hour. He was out of sight. Then he slowed down so McGarrity could catch up again. He kept slowing down, but he couldn't see McGarrity anyplace. Finally he turned around and slowly drove back about two miles. And there's McGarrity, up against a tree, uniform torn to pieces, his motorcycle smashed beyond repair. The young fellow jumps out of the car and with anguish on his face runs over to McGarrity and says, "McGarrity, what happened?" The Irish cop looked up at him and said, "The last time you pulled away, I thought me motorcycle stopped and I got off."

And then there is that old joke about the fellow up in Boston. He sees a new church being built and he wonders what the denomination is. He walks around one side looking for a sign and sees none. He walks around the other side and then on the back he sees a sign that says, "If you're tired of sin, come in." And some wag wrote under it, "If you aren't, call Hobart 4720."

Ladies and gentlemen, I always tell those two cornball jokes. I learned one thing well. Fundamentally, most of us are pretty much alike. You know when I told those jokes two nights ago in Chicago they didn't laugh any more or any less than you did tonight. I told the same jokes in London, England, and they too laughed just as much as you did tonight. You see it's really true—if, heaven forbid, you stick a fellow in the backside with a hatpin in Fort Lauderdale he'll jump about as far as a fellow in Chicago, Boston, or Enid, Oklahoma.

So as I talk tonight let's do one thing. Let's not hide behind that old Dorthea Brand alibi: we're different. I'm going to tell you the same story I tell every place I go. I won't change it for Fort Lauderdale. Oh, granted, somebody always grabs me by the shoulder just before I'm ready to go on and says, "Mr. Hipple, I don't want to tell you what to say, but the people down here are different." Well, what's different about them, I ask. Have they got a cleft head and walk on the left side of the street? They don't, they love and they laugh and they cry, like everyone else. I don't know whether you fellows in the audience know it or not, but girls are going over big on the West Coast, too. You take my word for it.

The first thing I want to do is show you some props I have up here on the stage. This is a bottle of ice-cold Coca Cola. It has six ounces of Coke in it. It sells for ten cents (pause); a buck at the Fountainbleau or at the Pump Room of the Ambassador East in Chicago. You know something rather interesting about it is: this bottle here that I'm holding in my left hand is the same as the one I have in my right hand. And there is even another bottle here and it, too, is the same. I know it's hard to believe, but they all have the same amount of Coca Cola in each bottle.

And it's amazing, but when they advertise Coca Cola, they never say anything different for Fort Lauderdale. They tell the same message in New York and Boston and Cleveland: "Drink ice-cold Coca Cola—it's the real thing."

I'll put these down and show you something else. This here? Ajax, that foaming cleanser—chases the dirt right down the drain. They all have this little piece of paper on the top to cover the pre-punched holes. I personally checked and found that this can of Ajax in my left hand has the same number of holes in the top as this other one sitting on the table. And they both have the same red letters, AJAX. If you brought in ten thousand cases they'd all look alike and all sell for the same price.

Tide! Tide's in—dirt's out! This box of Tide I'm holding up says it's a washday miracle, and darned if they didn't print the same thing on these other two on the table. Yes, they all have the same amount of Tide in each box.

Did I hear some of the older people in the audience say, "What happened to the Gold Dust Twins? For you young people, it was advertised on the back cover of every *Saturday Evening Post* through the first fifteen to eighteen years of my life. And then they cut back on their advertising. They're dead as a mackerel now. You can stop telling the public about your product any time you want and the day you stop telling them, get ready to cut your neck from ear to ear. You're through!

What really interests me most about these products I've shown you is that some stores sell infinitely more cans of Ajax, or more bottles of Coca Cola, or more Tide or more watches or whatever you want to pick out, than others do. Why? You see I'm just nutty enough to believe that the difference, the split difference, between success and failure, is advertising and merchandising.

And then you say to yourself—you satiated sales people who have been in selling all your life—"How big a fool does this man think we are? Because, my dear Mr. Hipple, price makes the difference."

Really? You mean price is the determining factor in why people buy? It's a good thing I came to Fort Lauderdale, because, for your information, according to *Fortune* magazine, which is unerringly right, "Only 4 percent of the people in the United States buy price. We sell price to the other 96 percent."

If we have to, we get the customer by the collar and yell, "Look, I have this item for $49.95. I don't want to trade you up, just buy this item I advertised."

Do me a favor, will you? The next time you go out to buy an automobile, wire me at McLean, Virginia, and tell me how it worked out. I want you to walk into a Ford, Chevy or Plymouth showroom and grab the salesman under his armpits and get him up on his feet. Then tell him you want to buy a car. His little eyes will light up like coals. Tell him you want a black Ford, Chevy, or a Plymouth depending on what showroom you are in. Tell him you want a straight stick. Just as he gets ready to write up the order say, "Before you start writing, I want to tell you something." He'll panic and say, "You're not going to cancel?"

"No, but before you write I want to tell you what I don't want on the car. I don't want an automatic transmission, I don't want power brakes, power steering, a radio, an air conditioner, a water bag to squirt water on my windshield, whitewall tires and I don't want..." He's ready to throw up on you.

"What do you want?" he asks.

"I just want a black car with a straight stick."

Now folks, don't you think if you practiced real hard you could do what I just said? If you do, I'll promise you a saving of five or six hundred dollars on the low end of the line. Not on what you drove over here tonight. Now you're talking twelve to fifteen hundred dollars. I'd like to ask a favor of my audience. Will all the people that drove to this sales rally tonight in a totally stripped car—will you all stand up together so I can show you to the rest of the audience? Nobody? You're kidding me. You didn't go for all that extra stuff did you? I thought you wanted price? Didn't you know that the stripped car would go just as fast as the one you're driving? Didn't you know it would last just as long and you'd be infinitely safer because you wouldn't be playing with all that jazz? Now think about it. You can save around fifteen hundred dollars that you pay tax on if you'll just ask for the price! I'll tell you what you bought. You bought the *difference*. It's the only sanctuary left in selling.

Now to pacify me so I don't become violent, accept what I say. And let's talk about the fact that I told you it was my considered opinion that advertising and merchandising were the fastest road to success. It's the most powerful medium in the world for moving people. It's legion what it will do. You can do almost anything you want with the consuming public with advertising: newspaper advertising, television, radio, magazines, direct mail—day in and day out—advertise and you move the world.

Remember, I told you those jokes in the beginning? Not just to pass time, but to prove we're all pretty much alike.

You're like me. You get up every morning. We're bitter about it, but we do get up. We stagger into the bathroom and wash our face with our nationally-advertised soap, and then we men shave with our nationally-advertised shaving cream and razor. And of course we have to brush our teeth, or what's left of them, with our nationally advertised toothpaste. We couldn't go to work with our hair looking like that, so "A little dab will do you" (not two, we don't want the girls in the office chasing us). And they have explained to us men that we smell, too. I'm glad my daddy is not alive today to know his son is using a deodorant. I am; it's just a case of whether it's Right Guard or Left Guard, I'm using it. After that's all over, we go downstairs to drink our coffee with the forty-three beans and smoke our cancerous cigarette in a flip-top box.

A dentist told me, "Worthington, I give you my solemn word, you could wash your teeth better with salt." Now the only question is: Have you got the guts to tell your friends you're using salt instead of toothpaste? Please believe me when I tell you, when you invite people over to your house to a cookout or to play bridge, and they finally go into your bathroom and lock the door, they look in your medicine closet. How do I know that? We look in theirs; what makes you think they don't look in ours? Yes, it works. We live on advertised products. But I have actually had people tell me that advertising doesn't work for them. For years I used to carry a Coke bottle around with me because I always wanted to shove it down their throat the hard way—bottom up.

So that you can all get home to make the late show, will you accept what I've told you about advertising? It will do the job, but you have to take it in your arms and love it. Don't ever fight it. The more you do, the more you'll sell. Why, I tell people if they only have one truck, to wash it up, paint number 7 on it and drive it all over town! Put your name as many times as you can in front of the consuming public. It's tough to even do bad advertising as long as you keep your name in front of the public. Remember, familiarity disarms opposition. If they hear your name enough times you could be a burglar and they'd say, "Let him in." I'm so sold that I really believe if you advertised water buffalo ears enough, and put them in a cellophane bag, some guy would walk in and say, "I'll take a package of those water buffalo ears." What he will do with them I haven't the slightest idea, but he'll buy them.

Because advertising works so well, on any given day you want to pick, a live prospective customer walks into the store. Now something happens that no living man since the beginning of time has been able to overcome or hardly even to describe. This customer, who was driven in by the force of millions and millions of dollars worth of advertising, now finds himself face to face with a phenomenon nobody can explain. If you put your hands on this phenomenon he's warm; he's in a vertical position. They call him a salesman. What this man can do in a split second is beyond belief. He can blow a million-dollar advertising campaign faster than anybody in the world. He's a symphony at this. You'd think he went into training. After he has lost the customer and the boss asks him what happened, he's safe. He's safe because one word in the English language saves him—that word is SHOPPER. What this poor man doesn't understand, is that everybody is a shopper. Did you ever hear your wife say, "I'm going out buying, Arthur." Not on your life. You'd kill her, so she says, "I'm going shopping." Later she comes back carrying so much it would rupture a man, but I guess women don't get ruptured.

Not so long ago one of the watch companies, the Elgin Watch Company, brought out a new watch. They thought it was a tremendously good thing. It had what they called a dura-mainspring—you couldn't wind it too tightly. Many people broke their watches for this reason. They sent shoppers out to see how their watch was selling. One shopper walked into a big store, and the clerk was very nice. He put the watches out. (They don't talk much. They don't bother you if you don't bother them.) The shopper looked the watches over for quite awhile, and then he picked up one of the Elgins and another watch and asked the clerk what the difference was. The clerk took the two watches in his hand, turned them over and said, "Eleven dollars and fifty cents."

Kill him, kill him! He believes it. Ask what's the difference between that car and this one over here and the auto salesman will give you about the same answer. "Two hundred and seventy dollars, sir. It says so right here on the sticker."

This type of selling is destroying us. It's killing something we need so badly today. We have to have him, we can't do without him. We've told him the whole economy, like the burden of Atlas, rests on him. We need him for the most important reason in the world—the one Jack Lacy talked about—the fact that half the people buy, but we have to sell the other half. We need him TO MAKE A SHOPPER INTO A BUYER.

We support him with all kinds of advertising. We give him spec sheets with all the information. He doesn't read it. If he does he forgets most of it, and at the crucial moment when he could kick the sale over he doesn't have the facts at his finger tips.

There is a man in this audience tonight from Bell Electric. He deserves an orchid. What this man knew about the new Tappan Electric range, which I wanted to get, was fantastic. He's a throwback, a much older man. You don't find too many of them anymore.

And to think all we're asking the salesman to do is tell a story, sell the benefits. Don't get too technical. Let me show you a poster I have up here on this easel. You folks in the back can't read it. I'll read it for you. It says, "Last year one million people bought quarter-inch drills—not because they wanted one million quarter-inch drills but because they wanted one million quarter-inch holes." Again, sell it for what it will do for them.

Exposure sells. If you don't want to sell tombstones, I tell dealers, don't put one in your window. If you do I'll guarantee you someone will walk in the next day and say, "Uncle Otto passed on yesterday, his ticker, yeah—we need a stone." Believe me, it works. What the eye sees the eye buys. Woolworth's, Kresge's and Grant's—all those people and more—built empires on exposure. There's no magic to it. That's why I think so many people who come to these sales rallies are disappointed. They think they're going to come to a meeting like this and come away with the big secret: some strange new thing that will change their whole life. Sales people don't need new rules. They need to learn the old ones and apply them.

You know how good business is going to be this year? As good as you make it. Does that make you want to die a little? Put the monkey right back on you.

Before we leave each other tonight we must understand why there is all the poor selling, how we got the way we are. Have you ever wondered how people become salesmen? I made a study of it.

I'll never forget the first time I asked a man how and why he became a salesman.

"Well, Mr. Hipple," he said, "I used to play in an orchestra, to be honest with you, and one day they disbanded."

"Oh," I said, "and then what did you do?"

"I was out of work for a long time. I used to go down to the union hall every day, but there was no work for a sax player. It was my wife. She got tired of me sitting around the house and said, 'Harry, why don't you go out and get a job?'"

"Like what?" I said.

"There's all kinds of ads in the newspaper for salesmen. You don't have to have any experience. It seems as good as anything else."

"How long have you been at it?" I asked.

"Twenty-eight years," he answered.

EVERYONE MUST TRAIN

Again, how do you become a salesman? Why do you become a salesman? How about a doctor, a lawyer, a banker? How many years do these men have to train? Oh," you say, "that isn't fair Mr. Hipple." In other words, I shouldn't count those types of jobs or professions? Suppose I pick something that you might look down your nose at. How about a bricklayer or a lather? Do you want to take some of those on? How long do you think it takes to become a journeyman plumber? A master plumber? So long it would frighten you. And you'd better hope he learned his lesson well when he shows up at your house and you're standing in water up to your navel. And what would you think if he looked around and said, "I missed school that night. If you can swim over to the stairs I'll pull you out."

Oh, yeah, everybody has to train for what they do, but they forgot about the selling profession. After what I call a very brief training we're sent out to sell the world. Most salesmen don't even want to come to sales meetings. They might miss their favorite TV shows. According to the records there are over 9,000 books on salesmenship in the Library of Congress. Ask yourself how many you've read, how much time you've spent learning your profession. And last but not least, ask yourself if you'd want a doctor to operate on you or a lawyer to defend you in a murder case with the same amount of training as you've had. The winners we've talked about are the ones who have made that special effort to know selling from A to Z.

Well, it's easy to stand up here and rail about what we do and don't do. But it's the reason we all came tonight.

So we're here to get some new ideas, to recharge our batteries; to go out and do a better job tomorrow and tomorrow.

Before I leave you, I want to tell you a true story—a story I want you to remember all the rest of your lives. And it won't make any difference what business you're in—it applies.

About ten years ago, I was lying in my twin bed, and my wife was lying in hers. I turned to her and said, "Laurette, I notice they're making the print in the newspapers and magazines smaller."

She didn't even look up; she said, "You need glasses."

For better or for worse, for richer or poorer, for two bucks you've got a genius in the bed next to you. I didn't pay any attention to her and about a week later I walked into a wall. I waited a while longer and one day I said to her, "You know, I think I'll go see an eye man, preventive medicine. I might need glasses." She let me get away with it. If you men in the audience don't know, your wife knows she is going to live about twenty to thirty years longer than you for openers. Might as well throw the old boy a bone. "Have another piece of butter, Charlie." A little cholesterol will help you on the way.

Well, I went to see Dr. Rogers in Evanston, Illinois. He put me in the chair, had the dials going around, and when he was finished he said, "Mr. Hipple, you need glasses. That'll be $35."

I didn't tell this doctor that my wife told me the same thing for nothing and with no equipment. I said to him, "Look, do I have to have glasses?"

"Oh no," he said, "you could get a seeing-eye dog."

"Well, if it's that bad, I guess you'll have to make me up a pair."

"All right," he said. "This is Monday, you come back on Friday."

I went back right on time. But I had a mental block about glasses. I have a twin brother, actor Hugh Marlowe. You can see him every day on NBC at three in the afternoon, if you don't work. He was the original Ellery Queen in the movies and you can also see him in most of the movies on the late, late show. When he was six years old he was cross-eyed. The doctor said, "We'll put glasses on him and it'll straighten his eyes out." I remember like it was yesterday that we used to call him four eyes. Glasses! They never did anything for anyone in the looks department, but it was better than having a seeing-eye dog, so I went back. For you people who don't wear glasses, I can't help you; your day will come. The eye doctor has a little white table that he places the glasses on to establish that the frames are straight. Man isn't built too well. One ear is higher than the other or the nose is over to the left. Satisfied with the glasses, he placed them on me. They always rock them back and forth to get them on just right. And then he said, "How do they feel?"

I said, "Just fine."

"Wheww! Boy, you look like a million dollars in those glasses."

"Well," I said, "thank you very much."

He took them off and saw where I wasn't built just right. He bent one of the paddles over some heat, squeezed the other end with a tweezer, polished the glasses again and put them back on.

"Now," he said, "how do they feel?"

"Just fine."

"Mr. Hipple," he said, "did you ever think of modeling glasses? The young executive type?"

I laughed and said, "No, I hadn't."

He said, "Mrs. Wilson, come in here, I want you to see Mr. Hip . . ."

I bought two pair of glasses! The last thing I wanted to be was trapped without a pair of glasses. The doctor was polishing up my glasses and was going to put them in a leather case. I said, "I'll wear them."

I floated out through the transom. There I was on Emerson Avenue watching the peasants with 20/20 eyesight who couldn't have glasses. I went home and yelled, "Laurette, where are you?"

"I'm in here," she said. "What happened?"

"I got the glasses," I said.

She took one look at me and said, "Worthington, you look like a million dollars in glasses."

I told her that was what the doctor said. I almost killed myself the first night. Did you ever try sleeping with glasses on?

Enthusiasm—it's the most contagious disease in the world. Look, I don't want you to go back tomorrow and jump up and down on the counters—I just want you to double your enthusiasm.

Walter Chrysler, who was pure genius, is the man who said, "Over any other attribute a man I hire must have enthusiasm." That's the kind of man who can galvanize other men into action. So I leave you now with this wonderful thought by William Randolph Hearst. I've had it printed on the wall of every office I've ever had. I live by it and so can you. Here's what he said:

"If you want the public to get excited about your product, first get excited about it yourself."

So "Sell Yourself Rich." Goodnight, and thank you.

(See Next Page for What You Can Do to Sell Yourself Rich)

WHAT YOU CAN DO TO SELL YOURSELF RICH:

1. <u>Don't</u> tell a joke unless you have a reason for telling it.
2. Use props every chance you get in making a presentation. Your audience will remember better through association of ideas.
3. Remember that price is not the determining factor of why people buy.
4. Use advertising and merchandising. They are the key wedges in motivating people to buy.
5. How did you become a salesman? Remember your motivation and see that you keep learning.
6. Be enthusiastic. Enthusiasm is the most contagious disease in the world. The more you put out, the more you get back.

Hammer Home the Difference

Chapter 29

---

1. Several ideas to motivate your customers.
2. Salesmen are the most maligned men in America.
3. Sell the difference.

ANNOUNCER:

THE BUSINESSMEN'S RECORD CLUB is proud to present one of the finest talks ever delivered to any sales group. The speaker has proved himself a dynamic salesman as well as a forward-looking and highly competitive sales executive. He is the author of a previously best-selling record of the month, entitled "Sell Yourself Rich." Formerly Eastern Sales Manager and Merchandising Manager for the famous Fedders Corporation, he is now retained as a Marketing Consultant to that firm. It is a pleasure to introduce G. Worthington Hipple.

Hello, salesmen, wherever you are. I like a giant crowd like this. An old pro told me once, "Hipple, always try and get a crowd of 1,000 people. When it's that big there will always be someone in the audience that agrees with what you're saying." And there are enough here today.

I had just about gotten to a point in life where I was willing to agree that most people were fundamentally alike when a fellow told me this true story.

The second-largest advertising agency in the country was doing an advertising campaign for Heinz tomato catsup. They ran full-page ads all over the country showing a very attractive waitress carrying a tray with a big hamburger on it and a bottle of Heinz tomato catsup to a man in a restaurant. The headline in the ad read, "JUST WHAT HE WANTED," and in the body of the ad it told how Heinz's tomato catsup was made. The tomatoes were gently squeezed instead of crushing the very life out of them, and for this reason Heinz's was just a little better than the others. The campaign was a howling success. So successful that the Canadian office called up and said, "Look, why couldn't we run that campaign in Canada?"

The New York office said, "No reason at all. We'll send you up the ad mats."

They did, and a week later Canada called again and this time they said, "When will you Americans learn that the Canadian people don't think like you do?"

New York said, "What's the matter?"

"We couldn't possibly use that headline 'JUST WHAT HE WANTED.'"

"Well," New York said, "You don't have to make a federal case out of it. You can change the headline, but keep the body of the ad the same, telling how the tomatos are gently squeezed instead of crushing the very life out of them."

Canada said, "O.K."

They ran the ad in Canada and the only thing they changed was the headline "JUST WHAT HE WANTED" to "HE GETS IT DOWNTOWN. WHY NOT GIVE IT TO HIM AT HOME."

Let's take a second to talk about salesmen. Let's talk about the most maligned men in America. Why, they keep telling all these jokes about us. I've been around a long time and I've never had anyone come up to me and say, "Worth, did you hear the joke about the engineer and the farmer's daughter?" They always say salesman. They never say, did you hear the joke about the first vice president and the farmer's daughter. We're always the butt of the jokes. This amuses me because salesmen are so important. We have been told time and time again that everything hinges on us. All is lost without us. Make no mistake about it. The success or failure of any company, large or small, in any town, city, or hamlet, depends on the money that circulates through it, and this will be in direct proportion to the amount of selling we do. Without selling I don't need the bookkeeper. Don't they understand that? I don't need any trucks, I don't need anything. Do you fellows think that management has any idea that we salesmen have got them by the throat like that? I don't understand why they don't let us run the company. We spend enough time on our coffee breaks talking about how they are screwing everything up. Then if they did, in about thirty days we could all go into bankruptcy together.

Samson slew ten thousand Philistines with the jawbone of an ass. And we lose that many sales every day through the same medium!

What are we going to do about Mr. Salesman? This man we kid so much about. We have all been done a terrible injustice because apparently nobody thought we needed training. I guess they thought we could pick it up by osmosis. We are quite unlike an engineer, or a CPA, an architect or anybody else. What a wonderful world if all salesmen were as well trained as CPA's, engineers and all those other people who have to go through college plus higher training, such as a doctor or lawyer. How fantastic it would be. We'd be able to sell the public so much stuff they wouldn't have enough places to store it.

THE IMPERFECTIONS OF MAN

I thought you would like to know that Darwin says man is an idiot. And Jung, who is a disciple of Freud, says that basically all men are dishonest. Now I'm not going to argue with Jung. I don't know for sure if he is right or wrong. But a man very high in the church told me that if the churches had all the money that we declared on our income taxes every year that they never got, they'd never have to ask for another donation! I am not as bitter as Darwin and Jung. I simply say man is rotten to the core and let it go at that.

If I were to write a book about man it would be titled, *Mr. Enigma*. He's really unbelievable. The inconsistency of man is appalling. Perhaps Darwin was being nice. We can't figure out anything that is going on down here. We can't balance the budget; we can't figure out the farm problem. We can't figure out integration, segregation; nothing can we figure out down here. But we want to go to the moon—and we did—to the tune of forty billion dollars. I live right outside of Washington, D. C., and I know how these fellows think. They simply say: we've screwed up everything down here, let's go up there and see what they're doing. And they will, they're manly little fellows.

What has all this got to do with sales? The reason I've taken the time to comment on the above is because before I tell you what I have to say, you must understand one thing well. The material we've got to work with is not so good. There is an element of human failure in all of us. We are to be pitied, coddled and helped, and I'll tell you one person who isn't getting enough help and that's the salesman. They say that your child is a product of your home and what you do. And I say that salesmen are a product of the company they work for. I wonder how sincere some of these companies really are? Is it just one of these annual ring-a-ding sales meetings? One of those conventions where we get our peas and chicken, listen to a lot of talking and then go home until next year? Where is the consistency? If, as I've mentioned before, we can't remember half of what we've heard eight hours ago, how are we supposed to remember for a whole year?

There has been a drastic change in our economy—in the marketplace. The rise and fall of so many discount houses has proven that that route was fraught with danger from its inception. The safest, surest route to more sales and more profit is *selling the difference*. As I've said many times in the past, selling the difference is the only sanctuary left.

Not so long ago, I went into a hardware store and said to one of the clerks, "I want to get a hammer, what have you got?"

He said, "I've got one here for $3.98."

"I don't want to build a church or anything like that," I told him. "I just want to knock in a few nails. Do you have anything less expensive?"

"Yes," he said, "I have one here for $1.98."

In a loose moment I said to him, "Tell me, what's the difference?"

And he told me, "$2."

I left and went to another store. The kid behind the counter had two kinds, like the first one I talked with, but in all honesty I must admit when I asked him what the difference between the two hammers was he told me they were both manufactured by Plumb; for you people in the audience who don't know, that's a company that manufactures hardware. I wouldn't be without that kind of information. I wanted to call my wife right away and tell her. I pushed on and went to a third store, and this is what happened, and it's a true story.

The same routine: I told the young man I wanted to buy a hammer; and before I could get my mouth closed on hammer, he had one in my hand. He said, "You can really get a grip on that, can't you?"

I said, "Yes."

He said, "Sir, that handle is made of second growth hickory. It'll stay smooth like that as long as you have it. You see that steel collar under the head?"

"Yes."

"That's 25 percent stronger than any other handle. With those fluted claws you can pull rusted nails or spikes, and you won't have to worry about them snapping off. You know sir, the measure of a good hammer is if it's a balanced hammer." With that he placed it on the counter to show me that it was perfectly balanced and then picked it up again. "Notice," he said, "that the head is sealed on, you'll never have to put any wedges in to keep the head on." And then he beat on the floor as hard as he could with the face of the hammer. "Sir, you can beat on case-hardened nails in cinder block and that double-dropped forged head won't pit. That's some hammer, isn't it?" he finished, and smiled.

"It sure is," I nodded, "but do you have anything a little less expensive?"

"You bet I do." He came back in a hurry. "I've got one here for $1.98." He held it out toward me and said, "Look out, don't drop it."

I asked, "Why?"

"Oh," he said, "it's a casting. You drop it on this cement floor and it's liable to break. This handle is made of southern pine, sir. If you keep it sanded real well, you'll keep most of the splinters out of your hands. Sorta feels like a hockey stick, doesn't it?"

I had to laugh and said, "Yes it does."

What's the difference between the two hammers? $2? Oh, no, no, no. This young man took the time to hammer home the difference. And from that true story I got the title for my second record.

Did you ever think by the wildest stretch of your imagination that a guy could talk that long about a lousy $3.98 hammer? Did you ever stop to think about all you could say about the product you sell if you took the time to always hammer home the difference? When you do, you'll find price starts to become secondary.

HOW TO FAIL WITH A BETTER MOUSETRAP

For you people in the audience in the back of the room, who want to be near the exits or quickly get to the men's room, take my word for it. What I have in my hand is a mousetrap. They're touchy little things. You have to be careful when you set them so that they don't pop up right in your eye. You put the piece of cheese in here like this and then set it. I was up in Montreal, Canada giving a talk for Kraft. I mentioned that you put a piece of Cracker Barrel cheese in the trap—they liked that. A mouse or a rat is like man. He's sneaky. He won't come when you're looking, but when you're not—pop! You've got a mouse. Now a man comes home and his wife screams, "Hubert, is that you?"

And he says, "Yeah; something happen to the kids?"

She says, "No. We caught a mouse."

He says, "What do you want me to do about it?"

She says, "Get rid of it." Do you see how she thinks. It's all right if *you* get the black death, but she wants nothing to do with it. If you're successful at what you're doing just throw the trap away, they're that inexpensive. If not, you gingerly get the mouse out and then burn the trap just enough so the other mouse won't know Dr. Kildare was here.

You wouldn't be without this information, would you? Is there anybody in the room that didn't hear from his dad or know all by himself that if you build a better mousetrap, they'll beat a path to your door? We've been using that old bromide for years. Let me tell you right now, it went out with high-button shoes and celluloid collars. I wanted your meeting to be a howling success so I brought you a better mousetrap. This one I'm holding is a stainless steel mousetrap. It's so simple to operate. You just put the piece of cheese in here and squeeze it. It's set and ready to go. It's also a four-way mousetrap. You'll catch him any way he comes. When you do, you don't have to wait until Hubert comes home. You just squeeze it like this and let the mouse fall out. It's a better mousetrap—make no mistake about it.

There's only one thing wrong. The company that made this

mousetrap went into bankruptcy. I'm serious. I knew one of the principals involved. The principals were living under the delusion that if you built a better mousetrap, they would beat a path to your door. Nobody will ever beat a path to your door. If you think you've got a better product, a better service, you've got to beat a path to *their* door.

To prove the point further, Schick came out with a new razor blade that would give you ten to fifteen more shaves per razor. Here is an ad right here in my hand that they ran full-page in *Life* and *Saturday Evening Post* magazines. And believe it or not, the lead line in the ad is, "We built a better mousetrap!" These people know they've got to *advertise* and *merchandise* any new product they put on the market. So copy the giants.

MARKET CHANGES

And you've got to be ready. One day a friend of mine called and told me he wanted me to give a talk for him. He said, "Worthington, this talk will be for the Clay Products Institute. We're not selling enough bricks—ones that we manufacture for houses and buildings."

I said, "You're kidding. You've got to be selling more bricks. They're building buildings and houses like a drunken sailor spends money."

"That's right, but too many of them are being built with glass, and in the houses out in the suburbs they're using USED BRICKS."

"Well, it costs less, is that why?"

"No," he answered. "They've run out of used brick, now it costs more for used bricks than new ones."

In short the brick people found themselves in trouble. I talked at their convention, where the theme was "Get Our Business Back." They did, too. They even started to manufacture used bricks.

Here's another example of how quickly a market can shift without any warning.

I want to be a success just like everyone else so I keep reading the *Wall Street Journal*, like they advertise. In the *Journal* I read an article telling about the gaslight comeback, and how this comeback brought rising revenues for one of the utility companies.

It seems that one day one of the men with the gas company was going over their inventory of equipment and found out that they had 80,000 gas lamp posts that they had been carrying since the turn of the century. They did an advertising and merchandising job on those old gas lamp posts like nothing you've ever seen. It became a status symbol to have one in front of your house. They sold the whole 80,000, and one local manufacturing company made a small fortune making copies of them. Well, how about the electric companies? Did they just throw up their hands and say, "The gas company was lucky"?

A spokesman for Commonwealth Edison Institute of Chicago said, "We started to advertise and merchandise our outdoor electric lights." A spokesman for the Georgia Power and Light Company had this to say about fighting the gas competition: "We started advertising that you can turn ours off and on from inside the house. You can have a brighter light with electricity; and, if that nostalgia of a gas light is what you want, we'll give you a little bulb that flickers just like a flame."

Hammer home the difference! That is what they were buying—not price, but the difference. People wanted used bricks even if they cost more. You couldn't shove new bricks down their throats. They wanted gas lamp posts. They wanted the difference.

THE CHALLENGE OF SELLING NEW PRODUCTS

I've pioneered in selling a tremendous number of new products. It's not easy. Remember, we established a long time ago, man isn't too bright. He's fought every new product that ever came down the pike. Man knew that the cotton gin wouldn't work, the steam engine would be a bust, you wouldn't be able to get an airplane off the ground, and, of course, the electric washing machine wouldn't work, to say nothing of appliances as silly as TV sets. At least we can say one thing about man. He's consistent. He's never been right yet.

When I first went with the Fedders Air Conditioning Company about four people in the country had air conditioners. Women were our biggest problem. They said they were too noisy and you'd turn blue in bed. The first thing I was out doing was getting dealers. I'll never forget one dealer. I really went to work on him. I told him there was almost total saturation in black-and-white TV, refrigerators, washers and dryers, and that air conditioning was the new crown prince of the appliance industry. I talked my head off about the benefits. The only thing I didn't have was the violins in the background. When I got all through the dealer looked at me kindly and said, "Mr. Hipple, you sure tell a terrific story, but we don't get any calls for air conditioners."

If he hadn't said what he did, I'd have dropped dead. That's why I always carry this box with me. It's about two feet long and six inches square. I've become a legend in my time because of this box. I always have it with me when I'm selling a new product. You walk into any dealer and stand there with this box under your arm and don't tell him what's in it, and it begins to bother him. I'm not advocating you do it in your bank. When that dealer said the same thing the dealers used to say to me when I was pioneering TV, I was ready for him. I said, "Mr. Charles, could I ask you a question?"

He said, "Yes, you're a nice young fellow." And I was then.

I said, "Mr. Charles, did anyone ever come into your place and ask you for a haircut?"

He waited a minute and then looked at me with his one good eye. "No," he said, "nobody ever came in here and asked me for a haircut."

I was fast in those days and before he could get his big fat mouth open again I flipped the top of the box open and pulled out a red, white and blue barber pole liner and set it on his counter.

"Mr. Charles, if you let me put this in your window, I'll lay you eight to five in two days someone will come in and ask you for a haircut—just give me the clippers on the side."

Let me ask every man in the audience a question. Is there a man in the room that ever ran into an appliance store twenty or more years ago and said, "Hey, if they ever invent television, let me know, I'll want one"?

It doesn't work that way. It never has and never will. If you don't display it, don't advertise it, don't merchandise it, you won't have to worry about getting any calls for it. The public aren't mind readers. You have to subject them to the disease. I didn't just tell you this story about the barber pole to jolly you up. You laughed and applauded enough, but to top it off, let me tell you this. Not long ago I was in New York giving a talk for Fedders. A young fellow came up to me after I was through and said, "Mr.

What's in the box?

If you put a barber pole in your store window, somebody will come in and ask for a haircut.

Hipple, I've heard every talk you ever made for Fedders. That story you told about the barber pole is priceless." I thanked him and he continued, "I own an appliance store in Queens. A couple of days ago a lady came in, and I said, 'May I help you?'

"She said, 'Yes, I'd like to get a feather duster.'

"I said, 'We don't sell feather dusters.'

"She said, 'I want one like you have in your window.'

" 'Oh,' I said, and looked in the window, 'We've been looking for that for two weeks, where is it?' "

Exposure: get it out where they can see it. All the giants built their empires on it.

TAKE A LESSON FROM SUCCESS

Not so long ago Arnold Palmer won one of the four Masters he has won. When he was walking off the eighteenth green, a newspaper man grabbed him and said, "Arnold, I wonder if I could have an interview with you?" Arnold's a very nice guy, so he said, "Yes, sir, but I wonder if you'll give me about forty minutes. I'll meet you in the club house."

And the newspaper man told me, "I watched the great Arnold Palmer walk over to the putting green and for a half an hour, putt!"

They say that 5 percent of the people playing golf break a 100. Do you know why we play so poorly? For the same reason we do a bad job at selling most of the time. In golf we go out on Sunday, take a couple of practice swings and away we go. The first hole a seven, then a nine, and it gets worse—not counting kicking and cheating.

Why do all the pros in any sport, why do all successful people, work hour after hour to better themselves? What makes us sales people think we don't have to do the same thing?

When you're through working today, ask yourself a question. "How generous can I afford to be with tomorrow?" And remember no matter where you go or what you do, someday life is going to present us with a bill, and it's a question of how well we do in life when it comes to paying it.

In my recording "Sell Yourself Rich," I tell you you can sell yourself rich, and now I add to it, you can, if you'll also "Hammer Home the Difference."

Thank you for being the perfect audience and good afternoon.

WHAT YOU CAN DO TO SELL YOURSELF RICH:

1. You can use the hammer story in this chapter with almost any sales group. Everytime I'm asked to talk to some national sales meeting the man that hires me always says, "You're going to be sure and tell the hammer story, aren't you?"
2. You might have the finest product on the market, but they still won't beat a path to your door. You have to beat a path to their door. One of your biggest helpers will always be advertising and merchandising.
3. Your product needs all the exposure you can get. Don't forget the old "Eye level is buy level." If you ever have a customer tell you he doesn't get any calls for a new product you've presented, then bring out the barber pole.
4. Practice, practice. Copy the pros. The reason you play lousy golf is because you don't practice enough. Know your presentation like the back of your hand. Be ready to counter any objections the customer might bring up.
5. Be sure and use the produce analysis sheet in this book (see p. 171). On one side list possible objections. On the other side of the page list logical answers—not when you get to the customer, long before you get to the customer.

Professional Selling from A to Z

Chapter 30

---

1. You can apply the selling techniques put forth in this chapter to selling any product.

THIS CHAPTER CERTAINLY HAS TO BE ONE of the very best sales guides ever developed by any man. It's so good I've told many it's worth the price of the book alone.

It was written by Mr. W. R. Johnston, the Director of Sales for Mallinckrodt, Inc., of Hazelwood, Missouri. Bill Johnston has given me permission to print it word for word as he wrote it.

For anyone selling in the medical field it speaks for itself, but how about you? You sell life insurance, boats, cars, bowling balls, or something else. You'll never find anything better. All you have to do is just put your product in the place of the Mallinckrodt product.

Mr. Johnston says it very well on his second page and I quote, "There are some basic laws that govern good selling regardless of the nature of the product."

You have a real treat for yourself when you come to Mr. Johnston's FAB method which goes over the facts, advantages and benefits of *your product*. This will also include his P-A-C-E-S meaning, performance, appearance, convenience, economy and safety.

Now I've said it enough times in this book, but I'll say it again: "I not only use all the brains I have, but all I can borrow" (Woodrow Wilson). Start borrowing.

PROFESSIONAL SELLING
THE MALLINCKRODT WAY
By W. R. Johnston

WHAT IS A PROFESSIONAL SALES REPRESENTATIVE? Without a doubt, every company in the pharmaceutical industry has its own definition. As far as Mallinckrodt is concerned, a Diagnostic Sales Representative and salesman are one and the same—the only exception being that we feel the term Professional Salesman or Professional Sales Specialist is more adequate.

Some people associate the word salesman with a cigar-smoking, desk-pounding loudmouth with a horse blanket for a sport coat. Perhaps this holds true in some types of selling, but certainly not Diagnostic Selling.

As a Mallinckrodt Diagnostic Salesman, you are calling on some of the most highly educated men in the world, many of whom are world-renowned authorities in their field. As a Mallinckrodt salesman, you are selling them the most important commodity in the world—you are selling health and a means to human happiness.

All of us want two things out of life—success and happiness. What does success mean to you as a Mallinckrodt salesman? The answer is obvious. You want to have work that is both enjoyable and worthwhile, with an income that will enable you and your family to enjoy a good life. You want recognition and advancement. Happiness is not obvious, but certainly the man who is doing his best in his territory has a better chance of being happy than one who is doing just enough to get by.

Mallinckrodt offers many things, among them a reputation for integrity and honesty that has been evidenced for many years now. Mallinckrodt offers an entree into the offices of the busy specialist, the hospital and laboratories, not to mention X-ray dealers and medical suppliers. Mallinckrodt offers the prestige of being the leader in the field of diagnostics and radiopharmaceuticals plus being a pioneer in chemicals and various other forms of research which are recognized throughout the world. Mallinckrodt offers membership on a team that will last for many, many years with an opportunity for advancement, work that is interesting and educational, and a good living for you and your family. As a member of the Mallinckrodt Team, it will be your job to perpetuate the excellent name of Mallinckrodt and to sell its products. Actually this type of selling is considered as tangible selling, but it is really *intangible tangible selling.*

Although orders are written and agreements made, most new sales are based on evaluation. Consequently, your intangible tangible type of selling is based on getting the physician or technician to try the product, following up the results of the evaluation, then securing the sale. This chain of events is a reflection on your ability as a salesman. As stated before, diagnostic selling to the doctor in his office or the hospital is salesmanship of the highest caliber, directed to the most intelligent and best educated prospect in the sales field. No place in the sales field are appearance, intelligence and knowledge more essential than in diagnostic selling.

BASIC SALES TECHNIQUES

There are some basic laws that govern good selling regardless of the nature of the product, type of prospect, or when the sale is made. On this foundation, diagnostic selling should be planned. In selling your product, these principles are used. You should incorporate them into the well-planned sales structure.

Remember, diagnostic selling is a service to the prospect and not just a device for getting orders. It is the personal presentation of an item and idea to a doctor or technologist with mutual benefit and gratification. It is the problem of securing his permission to do him a favor.

Planning a sales presentation requires background information on your product, on competitive products, and on the prospect. To present a product to your doctors, that product must be clearly understood by you first. The purpose for which it is intended or the uses the product can fulfill should be clear in your mind. Know what benefits your product offers to the doctor and also know its limitations. In the case of diagnostic products, know the method of action or the pharmacology, be acquainted with the side reactions or toxicity, its stability, the literature, the packaging, and the price. Also familiarize yourself with competition supplying similar products, not that you want to discuss the competitive product, but you probably can find some advantages in yours that will help you sell in the face of competition.

People like recognition. We're all egotists at heart. So when you call on a doctor, be sure and say "Doctor Jones." Don't use the term "Doc" or "Doctor." It doesn't have any individuality. However, don't get into the habit of opening every sentence with Doctor Smith this, and Doctor Smith that. In other words don't overuse the word "Doctor." The same thing applies to other members of the health service team. Call the technologist by name—first names are fine if they suggest it. Be sure you know the name of the technologist in the department. Remember that they are a barrier you have to pass if you are going to get into the inner office or lab, and the more friendship you can develop there, the better opportunity you have of saving time and getting interviews.

People buy because the product or service means more to them than the money involved. If you have a product that is new and there is no competition and it answers a long waited need, no salesmanship is necessary. But if the product has been on the market for some time and there is competition, if new uses have to be created, then salesmanship or motivation comes into the picture.

Why do doctors use certain preparations? Sometimes because of friendship with the salesman or the company. Today, however, due to increased competition and more salesmen in the field, this factor has less and less significance. A salesman who depends mainly on his friendship or personality for his business will have a sad awakening, because the doctor cannot pay his bills with your friendship. The majority of doctors will use a product because it works, not out of friendship for the salesman, unless, of course, the product is similar in efficacy.

PRESCRIBING MOTIVES

The most important reason for the doctor to use a product is that the product will be of more help in diagnosing the patient's illness; that is, the *product's performance* is superior in at least some way. Perhaps the reason is the *lack of toxicity* of the product, or the *safety* of the substance. Then cost enters into the equation. In many *instances*, it is the deciding factor. Of course, cost is often measured in ways other than dollars and cents; it could be measured in expenditure of time. *Another reason people buy is because of convenience or comfort.* Ease of administration is a convenience to the physician. *Sometimes appearance is a reason for buying*, such as the color, the taste, the odor—BAROSPERSE® could be a prime example.

We call these points *"buying motives,"* and in order that you can remember them, we have coined the word PACES—P standing for *Performance*, A for *Appearance*, C for *Comfort* or *Convenience*, E for *Economy* and S for *Safety*—PACES.

Probably the number one buying motive in our business is performance—what the product will do for the doctor and his patient. Number two might be safety—is the product safer for use in the various types of procedures? This is important, not only to the doctor, but for the patient. Number three might be convenience. For instance, many doctors prefer single or double dose IVP procedures to drip infusion, some prefer the individual dose cup of BAROSPERSE to measuring out bulk, etc.

Many of us place price in the upper category, but a national survey has shown that price is not always such an important consideration. *In a pharmaceutical survey of over 300 doctors, price ranked about fourth* in the reasons for buying a given product, and that was usually combined with some other buying motive.

Appearance would rank fifth. It is true that the appearance of a product may have some appeal, but something else is also very fundamental and you should remember that we are selling something doctors or technicians do not want. Doctors are not interested in buying vials, barium sulfate, isotopes, etc., as such. They are interested in buying what a good diagnostic agent will do. So our prime motive is to know what the product will do to help the physician more accurately diagnose his patients. Example: We don't sell CONRAY® as such, we sell the benefits and advantages of CONRAY—how CONRAY will help the physician diagnose his patient and how the physician can expect his patient to tolerate CONRAY.

Remember that in selling diagnostics, the product is secondary; we do not sell the product. We sell what the product will do for the doctor and how it will affect his patient. This brings us to product analysis, a division of our information into *F. A. B.—Facts, Advantages and Benefits.*

A *Fact* is a property or attribute of a product. It is a characteristic or trait that's actually part of the product. The chemical formula, size, color, or weight of a product are some of its facts. Facts tell something about a product.

An *Advantage* is what a fact does. Advantages describe what the facts do. Example: Our generator is completely self-contained; that's a fact. The advantage is that no in-laboratory assembly is required.

A *Benefit* is the value or worth that the user finds in a product. Benefits answer the question, "What's in it for me?", that Fact and Advantages don't answer. Example: The Fact that our generator has a greatly enlarged shield is a Fact; the Advantage is lower radiation levels surrounding the ULTRA-TechneKow® Generator; the Benefit that answers the question, "What's in it for me?", is less technical exposure and less interference with counting equipment.

To analyze a product, first consider the facts. Arrange these according to the PACES. The next step is to list the advantages derived from the facts. The last important step is to list all of the benefits the advantages will give to the customer. The benefits are the facts and advantages translated into what the customer really buys. Since he buys according to certain motives—the PACES—the benefits must be listed according to these motives.

Take each fact. Write all of the advantages and benefits that each fact offers to the doctor, technician or the patient. This can be done on a piece of paper. (Note Figure I.) After listing all the benefits each fact and advantage gives, go through the list and write the buying motive after each benefit.

Our ULTRA-TechneKow has a new "Ion Control" process that is a *fact* worth mentioning to a physician or technician. The *advantage* is that it reduces aluminum ion levels so that they are essentially undetectable by normal laboratory test methods. The *benefit* is that there need be no concern about aluminum ion effects on various tagging procedures such as with sulfur colloid kits. This benefit means safety and convenience to the doctor, technician, and the patient.

There is a tendency on the part of most men to talk about facts regarding the product. This is not the important consideration. It's what the product will do for the doctor or patient that is important—and that is what we should sell when we are talking

Figure 1.
F.A.B.

	FACTS	ADVANTAGES	BENEFITS
PERFORMANCE			
APPEARANCE			
CONVENIENCE			
ECONOMY			
SAFETY			

F.A.B.

FACT	ADVANTAGE	BENEFIT
Completely self-contained.	No in laboratory assembly required.	Saves technician time and eliminates errors.
Push button operation.	Simple and fast.	See above and provides low technician integrated dose.
Needle changed daily.	Eliminates possible contamination.	Assures sterility.
Fractional Elution vials available.	Allows for concentration elutions.	Makes bolus injection practical.
Sight Glass Elution safe.	Allows viewing of the elution process without increasing exposure.	Assures completion of elution; no blind milking.
Greatly enlarged lead shield.	Lowers radiation levels surrounding the Ultra-TechneKow.	Less technician exposure. Less interference with counting equipment.
500 ml saline supply.	Allows multiple elutions.	Multiple elutions increase total ^{99m}Tc yields.
Self aligning milking station.	Simple and fast.	Saves technician time and eliminates errors.
Ion control.	Reduces aluminum ion levels so that they are essentially undetectable by normal laboratory test methods.	No concern about aluminum ion effects on various tagging procedures such as with sulfur colloid kits.

about products. Facts are necessary, but they should be bolstered by the advantages and benefits that can be obtained from a product. I think you'll find that any product will have facts, and you can find two or three advantages or benefits for each fact. Try this out and see how many benefits you can find for our products. Also, compare competitive products to ours by the PACES—FAB method. It will help you in your work.

DEVELOPING A SALES PRESENTATION

While it is true that your presentations are not planned for you, it is felt that an outline should be followed in order to keep things in their proper perspective. Organization in a sales presentation is of vital importance. To help you do this, we have developed what we call the Seven Point Selling Formula. (Note Figure II.)

I. *The Greeting* is a means of getting the prospect's attention. For instance, you say, "Good morning, Doctor Brown." And you say this as if you mean it.

II. *The Compliment* can be used where indicated. I call this a softening agent. If the doctor or technician has written an article for a medical journal, it doesn't do any harm to tell him that you have noticed it and you consider it a very fine presentation. Or if he has given a talk before a medical or technician society, he likes to have that recognized. But don't use the compliment all the time—just where it is indicated and certainly not in terms of flattery.

III. *Creating Interest* with the physician or technician is of the utmost importance. It gives them, in a few words, the reason for your visit. An example might be, "Doctor Timpe, I can now offer you a new thyroid function test that is an exclusive procedure which indicates status of metabolically active thyroxine with a single test. It's clinically proven and reliable." Certainly the physician or in most cases the technician is going to be interested in the fact that it is new and also in the advantage that it is reliable.

IV. *Have your Facts, Advantages and Benefits* listed so that you can give them in relation to his needs. The "Interest" part is the most important benefit that the doctor can get from the use of the product, and that should be considered in relation to the type of product you are presenting and the procedure it is used in.

173

Figure II

SEVEN POINT PRESENTATION FORM

Dr._____   SPECIALTY   PRODUCT

  I *GREETING*

 II *COMPLIMENT*

III *CREATING INTEREST OR ATTENTION*
(Promise him something) crystallize a specific diagnostic need or problem in the doctor's mind. P-A-C-E-S

IV *FACTS, ADVANTAGES AND BENEFITS*
Desire for Mallinckrodt product. (Always give 3x as many benefits and advantages as facts.)

 V *PROOF–DEMONSTRATION*
Who says so? How do I know you're telling the truth—package insert, reprint, journal, etc.

VI *POINT OF AGREEMENT*
Draw out questions and objectives (Trial close). Pinpoint a P-A-C-E-S he's most prone to—would you agree, doctor, that our TechneColl Kit offers you and your technicians effectiveness and convenience?

VII *COMMITMENT*
(Close)—Will you use our ETR for your next several thyroid function tests and see how accurate and convenient it is to use?

COMMITMENT (cont.)   SPECIALTY PRODUCT

How many patients would you like to evaluate on our product and compare?
Obtain an evaluation (Commitment) when the doctor or technician commits himself to buy and use our product as diagnostic of choice, etc.

An atmosphere of conspicuous honesty must prevail during all selling situations.

If you are working VASCORAY™ with a cardiologist, obviously you would talk about its use in arch studies. If you are talking to a urologist, it would be about CYSTOKON®. Pick out the most important benefit as the interest-getter. The benefit the radiologist is getting from CONRAY in cerebral angiography is a better picture and a high degree of safety. The fact that our ULTRA-TechneKow +4 has more shielding means it's safer and protects the technologist from excessive exposure to radiation.

V. Some products lend themselves to *Demonstration*, and if you make the demonstration, have the doctor or technician take part in it. Let him help you do the demonstration. He'll remember it much longer if you will.

BAROSPERSE lends itself ideally to demonstration. Take 8 oz. of BAROSPERSE and add 5 oz. of water. At the same time have the technician or perhaps the physician do the same thing with a competitive barium sulfate. Shake both cups well and let the technician see for himself how well BAROSPERSE goes into suspension compared to the other. Then spread BAROSPERSE across the palm of your hand with your index finger and have the technician follow your example with the other product. The detail that BAROSPERSE shows as compared to the other product may be convincing evidence of BAROSPERSE's superiority. It must be remembered, however, that no matter how easy this demonstration seems, it should be practiced to make it perfect.

Also back up all pertinent claims about your product with *Proof*. Show the doctor in black and white how VASCORAY has helped other doctors. Show the physician, by the use of reprints, just how VASCORAY was used and worked for other radiologists. Don't make a claim unless you can back it up. The doctor may act like he believes you when you tell him something, but he'll remember your claim if you prove it to him in black and white. Let the other companies make verbal claims. We can show proof, so let's do it.

Reprints add believability to your presentation. Actually, you are introducing a third party into your sales story which can give you the leverage necessary to induce the doctor to buy or try your product.

Always show the reprint. Such information as the name of the article; the name of the journal where the article appeared; the context of the material such as highlights, conclusion or summary are of vital importance. If the reprint discusses studies, let the doctor know what kind—double blind, triple blind, cross-over, or random studies, etc. Nothing helps to sell a product like good third party reprints if described and shown correctly.

VI. *Next comes the Point of Agreement or Trial Close.* The question, *"What are trial closes?"* has come up. Trial closes are questions or statements used to determine the extent to which the doctor is sold. A trial close is used to get his reaction as to whether you should continue your sell or close the sale.

Trial closes should be planned and learned beforehand and inserted casually into the presentation. Find a point of interest in your story that you know the doctor will say *yes* to; make it hard for him to say no.

a. "You want your patients who are having an aortography procedure done to have the benefits of a product that will give them less patient discomfort, don't you?" Now close the sale or get a commitment. "Fine, Dr. Wallace, how many of your patients would you like to try on VASCORAY to see for yourself just what it can do?"

b. "Doctor, would you agree that the advantages that CON-RAY-30 offer you and your patient, particularly predictable results, make it worthwhile using in your practice?" The answer should be *yes* if he has been previously sold. If his answer is negative, you have to go back over the Benefits and find out where you missed.

Taking it for granted that he has been sold is a mistake. Only when he agrees with your trial close should you go on to the final step, the *Commitment.* Before we get into the different types of closes, let's cover another important point.

You can close at any point in a sales presentation; being able to recognize the opportunity comes with experience. For example, most technicians know about thyroid function tests, how they are used, the fact that they're all fairly accurate, but they don't all know the ETR^{TM} test or the difference in reliability between it and others, or the fact that it's not thrown off by steroids and pregnancy. You may have just gotten into your sales presentation when the doctor might say, "What is the difference between ETR and T3-T4 tests or how does your price compare?" or "Is the test easy to perform?" Any of these types of questions are questions that you can close on, if you know the answer.

CLOSES

VII. *Commitment or Close*. The most important part of an organized sales story is the close. What good does it do if you plan a sales story and don't ask the doctor to buy? Five or ten minutes, perhaps even more, are spent building up the product all in preparation of obtaining a commitment from the doctor, and it's surprising how few salesmen ever ask for the order. Why? In some cases, it's because they're just plain scared. In other cases, it's because they assume that the doctor will buy or order.

In selling you can assume nothing. You can't assume the doctor knows about Mallinckrodt Diagnostics or assume that he knows our product line. One noted sales lecturer said that when it comes to closing a sale, there seem to be too many colorful salesmen (yellow), afraid to ask for the order.

Closing is asking for the order and securing it. The sale is closed when you get the doctor's promise to use your product. It is not closed if you don't. Closing the sale is the reason for your employment. Your salary is given for closing sales. It is of the utmost importance that you know all you can about closing the sale.

Out of every call you make on a physician during a week, how many do you close? Let's get into the various types of closes.

a. Probably the most simple and most seldom-used close is *just plain asking the doctor to buy*. Although this is amateurish, it's better than no close at all.

b. *The Challenge Close*—Asking the doctor to compare the diagnostic results of CONRAY-400 against any other contrast media he is using. To be more specific, if the doctor claims that he has just started to use Hypaque M75 or Renografin 76, you might say: "That's fine, Doctor. Since you already believe that high iodine content is necessary, I would like you to try CONRAY-400 and compare the results you get against Hypaque or Renografin. I'm sure you'll find that our product will give you what is considered a better film study that will be a real improvement for you over what you are now using."

c. *Specific Number of Evaluations Close*—"Doctor, how many patients would you like to try on CONRAY-30 drip infusion for your IVPs? Fine, then I'll send you enough to evaluate them or I'll let your technician know that they are being sent and also explain the benefits of CONRAY-30 to him. I'll check back to see what your conclusions are after you try it. I'm sure you'll like it."

    d. *Assumptive Close*—"Doctor Nixon, with your permission I'm going to send you a supply of our b.e. bags to try on your patients for whom you want exceptional results and convenience for your next barium enema procedure. This way you'll be able to judge, at our expense, the value of our b.e. bag. I'll check back with you in a few weeks to find out the results. Do you feel that the amount I'm going to send you is enough to provide you with the opportunity to properly evaluate BAROSPERSE b.e. bags?"

    e. *Closing on a Benefit*—"Since you have agreed that you're interested in a product that has less side effects, particularly nausea, and I've proven to you that CONRAY has less, let me send you enough to evaluate on patients so you can judge for yourself."

    f. *Alternate Close* "I can appreciate the fact that you're satisfied with the product that you're now using. But would you agree that there are very few products that are completely tolerated by everybody? Would you consider using CYSTOKON so you can judge for yourself how well it's tolerated? Then you could compare it to the product you are now using and make your own decision as to which causes the less reaction."

    g. *The Ego-Building Close*—"Doctor Agnew, this product has been thoroughly documented, but let me leave you enough stock packages so you can run your own clinical trial. This way you can find out for yourself the benefits that VASCORAY will give you and your patients."

    h. *Choice Close*—"Doctor Timpe, you have your choice of CONRAY products to use in IVPs—CONRAY, CONRAY-400, VASCORAY, or our new drip infusion, CONRAY-30. Which do you prefer to order?"

    There are various types of closes. You, no doubt, have a pet close of your own. The important thing to remember is ask for the order; make sure the doctor commits himself to try the product. Actually, you're a highly trained professional salesman and it's vitally important to close the sale; otherwise, it was a waste of your time and the doctor's time. The physician sees all types of salesmen day in and day out. They know why you're calling on them. They can tell a good salesman from a poor one. The salesman who is prepared knows all about his product and competition. The salesman who plans his story and convinces the doctor that his product is superior is the salesman who wins the doctor's respect and the orders.

The Seven Point Sales Presentation is a good skeleton to follow. It helps put the horse in front of the cart. We don't send out planned presentations, but we do expect you to put your story in a logical pattern. The best way to do this is to sit down and write out a story until you're convinced what you're reading is a story that will sell. This will help you organize yourself so that you're not talking off the top of your head. Try your story out on a few doctors. If it works, use it.

If it doesn't, revamp it until it does. Practice your sales presentation on your wife or into a tape recorder. Listen to how you're selling, are you convincing? Does your wife feel your story makes sense? Practice makes perfect is an old saying, but it still holds true.

It is suggested that you follow the Basic Material sent to you during the promotional periods. This material contains the guidelines around which your presentation must be formed.

THE DIRECT APPROACH DETAIL

There are other methods of medical selling; there are situations where you can't use the *Seven Point Sales Presentation*. After you have made repeated calls on the same physician, your approach has to change a little. Even on initial calls, the *Question Approach or Presentation* or *Direct Approach* can be used. As with the Seven Point Sales Presentation, the Greeting, Compliment, are the same, but you can get right at the meat of the subject with a few well-placed questions. Example:
1. "Doctor, do you use drip infusion for IVPs?"
2. "Would you mind telling me which product you prefer to use for this procedure?"
3. "Is there any particular reason why you use this product?"
4. "Have you used CONRAY?"
5. If the answer is yes, follow with, "Were you and your patients satisfied with the results?" If the answer is no, ask why—if the answer is yes, ask, "Why don't you still use it?"

6. "With your permission, I would like to compare the product you're now using with CONRAY-30."

There is a multitude of questions you can use in the Direct Approach Presentation; however, ask them in a friendly indirect manner; let the doctor or technician express himself.

The *Direct Approach Presentation* gets you to the point right away. Your Point of Agreement or Trial Close and Commitment will be the same, of course. With a limited number of products, a few men have brought up the subject—what more can you say after you have seen him on the same product so many times? This is where experience comes in. You can tell the physician about experiences that some of his colleagues are having with the product. You can ask him questions about the product (build up his ego). Articles from medical journals, reprints, etc.—many ways can be thought of to keep the door to the physician open to you call after call. The important factor to remember in this situation is always to ask for the order. There are various and sundry ways of doing this, even to your best users, without perturbing him. Whatever you do, don't get into the habit of being a stock package dropper-offer. Admittedly, this has to be done at times, but always insist on giving them to the doctor personally, where possible, or to the technician when you know he can use them and has the ability to influence the doctor to OK the use of them. The personal touch with a good story and a strong close are of the utmost importance in this business. This can never be accomplished by dropping off samples. The U. S. mail and Western Union could do that for us if that were all that needed to be done. Selling is full of platitudes and slogans, but the one that states "plan your work and work your plan" is still of the utmost necessity in the highly specialized art of medical or diagnostic selling.

OBJECTIONS—HOW TO HANDLE THEM

Objections are a basic part of any sales interview. In fact, if objections or questions don't arise during your sales presentation, your prospect isn't listening, or else you're not making your story interesting enough to make him want to listen.

First of all, the best way to overcome an objection is to anticipate it. Since we have only a limited line of products to be concerned with, we have an opportunity to learn our product inside and out. The product analysis sheet (Figure III) is a convenient way of analyzing our products. Write down every possible objection that you can think of in the *Possible Objection* column, then look up the *Logical Answer*. Most of the objections that come to mind can be answered by the careful study of our package insert, medical literature, etc., or even the package itself. Write the *Logical Answer* to the question in the space across from the objection. Any subsequent question that arises in the physician's office that you can't answer, write down as soon as you leave his office. Then find out the answer from someone who knows (your regional manager, the R&D Department, etc.). This is a way to acquire a list of answers that will give you a stone wall defense against any question or objection that may arise.

Webster defines an objection as "reason or argument presented in opposition." To any salesman, an objection should be considered the doctor's way of saying, "I'm not yet ready to buy, I'm not sold."

Behind every objection—honest ones—is Fear. The physician fears the consequences of making the wrong decision. We may call it a lack of confidence, or doubt, or reluctance to change, or some other name, but it is still fear. A good question to ask yourself is, "Just what is this doctor afraid of?"

Saying that an objection is a form of fear can also work in reverse. If the product isn't understood and a full knowledge of it retained, an objection would be a cause of fear to the salesman. Actually, there are two types of objection.

I. *Sincere Objection*—Where the doctor is really in search of an answer to a particular phase of the product. It could be a sincere objection or doubt that competition has imbedded in his mind. A veteran salesman should welcome the sincerely expressed objection. Objections are an integral part of the sales process. You must accept this fact in order to reach a sounder philosophical basis on which to approach them.

Before answering an objection:

1. *Listen Carefully*—Make sure you understand what the doctor is objecting to. You can never find out by trying to overcome the objection before he gets it out. *Listen.*

2. *Act Interested*—Let the doctor know that you want to hear his objection. Be sympathetic.

Figure III

PRODUCT ANALYSIS

POSSIBLE OBJECTION	LOGICAL ANSWER

3. *Never Hurry Your Answer*—Even though you may have anticipated the question and have the answer on the tip of your tongue, let the doctor feel that you're thinking about it.

4. *Restate the Question* (Reflective Question) in your own words. This not only lets the doctor know that you understand his question, but it also gives you time to gather your thoughts. An example might be: "I don't use BAROSPERSE because it doesn't do the job." You could restate that objection by saying, "Dr. Zarchy, if I understand you correctly, you are concerned with diagnostic effectiveness. May I ask why you don't feel it's effective?" Restatements can sometimes make the objection seem less important and clarify it to you and the doctor. This method can also help to pinpoint his real objection.

5. *Never Magnify an Objection*—Wordiness reduces the force of your answer and may confuse the doctor. A lengthy reply builds up an objection and gives it undue importance. Answer each sincere objection clearly, emphatically, and in a straightforward manner. Lingering too long on an objection is like holding a magnifying glass over it.

6. When you answer, *be positive*. Say it is or it has, never say it may or might be or might have been.

7. *Use Proof* wherever possible when answering an objection.

8. *Be Honest*—If you don't know the answer, be just as positive as if you knew it. Tell the doctor that you don't know the answer but will see what you can find out for him. Then go on selling! Above all, don't fake or guess at the answer.

A sincere objection is important to the doctor. It is a good sign, a natural resistance. If you answer promptly, he has more confidence in you and your product. *It is easier to answer an objection the moment it comes up; in fact, it's a must.* If you don't answer it on the spot, and tell him you'll answer it later, he'll lose interest and be concentrating on why you didn't answer it then. Therefore, when he objects, answer him promptly.

REMOVING OBJECTIONS INOFFENSIVELY

The following is taken from Wendell White in his book, *The Psychology of Dealing with People*.

"The removal of objectionable ideas is a very delicate procedure because it entails danger of wounding the individual's pride.

The slightest injury to another's self-esteem may become an insurmountable barrier to dissuading him from a position to which he has committed himself through word or through act. To succeed in getting a person to give up an idea one must frequently proceed in a manner that will safeguard the person's pride. There are several ways in which one can disparage an idea expressed by another person without offending him."

White then suggests, among others, the following ways:

1. By exonerating the person from any blame for expressing the idea that is objectionable. For example, this may be done by saying,
    a. "I see that I did not make myself quite clear."
    b. "I hope that you will not feel that way when I present you with all the facts."
2. By making a concession before taking exception to the objectionable idea. For example:
    a. "Under normal conditions you are correct in that opinion, however, if I can prove to you..."
    b. "Your suggestion has much to recommend it. But on the other hand..."
    c. "There is a lot of truth in your contention, but when you stop to think that..."
3. By either revealing a deliberate attitude regarding the idea expressed or suggesting that the prospect do so.
    a. "That is really worth considering."
    b. "Perhaps if I could show you what some of your colleagues are doing in this case you might consider giving it a little more thought before deciding finally."
4. Either by stating that there are others who agree with the idea before disagreeing yourself or by agreeing and then raising a counter objection as an afterthought.
    a. "Young people often think that way. But after..."
    b. "I frequently hear the same thought expressed. But nevertheless, we feel that..."

Objections are requests for more information, as stated before, and objections should say to you, "I don't understand a particular part of the product well enough." When the doctor doesn't raise any objections, yet doesn't agree to order, or if he is hesitant about committing himself, he has a hidden objection that he has not disclosed. In a case like that you have to ask questions—try to find out why the doctor won't respond. A simple way of doing this is to ask why. Example: "Doctor Smith, what is the reason you won't use BAROSPERSE?" Another method is to say, "Perhaps I haven't made myself clear on some vital point that concerns you." The important factor is to pull the doctor's objection out into the open—then answer it. A good technique to use that most pros rely on is, after you have answered his hidden objective or any objection, to say then, "Dr. Smith, what is really bothering you about ETR? Isn't there something else you object to or want to know about my product?" The doctor is encouraged to reply with his real objection once he sees that he has not fooled you, or that you are really interested.

II. *Insincere Objection*—Most objections or questions that the physician confronts you with are sincere objections. In fact, you'll find that the objections you get in the majority of cases are Stock Objections or Questions and you'll pride yourself and impress the physician with your ability to answer them. Occasionally, you will run into a physician who will try to shoot you down with obstructions that can't or need not be answered. Usually a smile or quizzical look will brush aside an insincere objection. Questions and objections can be handled with knowledge, but *prejudice* is an altogether different hazard. If a man is prejudiced on a particular subject, most likely he has lived with it for many years and you're not going to change his mind in one call. Religion, politics, and a few other subjects are best to stay clear of. Besides the beforementioned obstacles in the pathway of making a sale, there lies one more type of hindrance which in some cases can give you a certain amount of trouble. It's the Stall. Example: "I'm too busy, I can't see you now, I'm just on my way to the hospital, see me later, I know all about your product. The price is too high. I'm satisfied with the product I'm using now." The only way to overcome a Stall is to get the doctor interested.

The easiest way to do that is to promise him something he wants, something you know he is interested in. Example: "I'm in a hurry—I can't see you now." "Doctor Diaz, busy men are my best customers because they know what they want. They recognize values and make quick decisions. Take a fast look at the product that will give you better pictures and at the same time cause less nuisance side effects. Here let me show you." You have complimented him, promised him something. That's how to start a demonstration! A *Stall* is voiced sometimes before you can start. "I'm not interested." One way you can answer it, "I understand why you are not interested now, but in a few minutes I believe I can show you why it would be in your best interest to consider using my product."

"I'm too busy now" is a frequent stall, and you can't get in. Don't argue! If it is possible for you to return later or in a day or two, ask for an appointment. Remember, treat each doctor as an individual. Don't be pushy or rude. Some physicians are busy and can't see you. If he has his hat and coat on rushing to go home or to his office—he's busy. Use good judgment when in a too-busy situation.

"See me later, I'm too busy now." How many times have you heard that reply? A good answer is, "I'm sorry you feel that way, Dr. McEwen, because if you didn't, I could show you a new thyroid function test that not only is accurate but easy to perform and reads through estrogens and pregnancy."

The magic touch is knowing when you can and when you can't apply these techniques. This, of course, comes with experience.

OVERCOMING THE PRICE STALL

Price is another stall, but it can be handled in various ways. Example: "It costs too much." Answer: "Doctor Duca, you feel it costs too much. Yes, it does seem expensive, but let me point out all the advantages you get."

Example: "Doctor Wallace, you would want to use an ULTRA-TechneKow generator that offers a higher degree of reliability, safety, and convenience to you, the technician, and the patient, wouldn't you?" "Yes, of course." "You use our generator and because of its enlarged lead shield you and your technician have lower radiation levels, and because of our ion control, you don't have to be concerned about aluminum ion effects on various tagging procedures, etc. Our pushbutton makes milking simple and fast. All this adds up to safety and convenience."

When the doctor says, "It costs too much," one man says the most effective method he has used is to stop talking, look at the doctor amazed and say, "What is cost, Doctor Harrigan?" When he answers, say to him, "I thought you meant cost in relation to diagnostic effectiveness for the patients." This is answering a Stall with a question. Tell the doctor if the product costs twice as much he would find it inexpensive if it gave a better picture and a higher degree of safety. Never make an issue of price. Remember, price is what the doctor or technician gives in return for the results the product gives him.

WANTMANSHIP

Doctors buy and use products because they help solve problems. The physician is only interested in using a product that is best for him and the patients, so it is not up to you as salesmen to create needs for the doctor; he already has them. You have to create Wantmanship. Wantmanship is your ability to verbally draw such an outstandingly vivid, motivating picture of your product that the physician will *Want* to use nothing else but *your* product for the procedure you have discussed with him. There are many pharmaceutical companies in the field today and thousands of salesmen out trying to get the business. For every procedure or function test, there are at least five or six products on the market that the doctor can use. Who is going to get the business? The salesman who is smart enough to make the physician want his product. The salesman who knows how to create Wantmanship.

How is Wantmanship created? By taking the *Facts, Advantages and Benefits* of a product, applying the *Buying Motives* (PACES), recognizing the product's advantages and the disadvantages, and being able to understand and answer every possible objection concerning the product. These factors, plus thorough knowledge of competitive wares lead to the ability to create Wantmanship. These are just the first steps, of course. To be a real professional salesman, it must be realized that to create Wantmanship, you must take all the above factors and boil them down to a good, logical sales presentation. A presentation that will make the doctor want your product for his patient. Why? Because of its superior performance or perhaps just because of the packaging that makes the product more convenient. The benefits of a product, your ability to procure total knowledge of the product, and salesmanship all add up to build the power that creates Wantmanship.

PLANNING YOUR WORK

A great deal of time can be saved and a lot of confusion avoided if you plan your work. The man who plans his work and keeps all his records up-to-date, answers letters from the home office and his regional manager, is well organized. Keeping your records up-to-date and planning your calls a night or a week in advance helps to enhance your productivity and can make more money for you. You must remember in your territory, you are in business for yourself, and you are Mallinckrodt as far as your customers are concerned. If you were self-employed, it would be essential for you to keep up your forms and reports. It is just as essential that you do it while working for Mallinckrodt. By planning your work, I mean that each night you should make a schedule of the doctors and/or hospitals you are going to call on the following day. You should analyze the needs of the people you are going to see so you can talk to them intelligently. Arrange your calls so as not to do too much unnecessary driving; and in order to get as complete coverage as possible, allocate your calls per day.

If you have kept good records, you will know what to talk about when you call on your doctors from day to day. You will know the hospital requirements. There is only one way in the world to have this information, and that is to keep your records up-to-date.

Often you are asked by your regional manager or the home office for information. Be sure and take care of this at once. Don't postpone it. The man who has difficulty with his records, reports, etc., is the man who defers them until the end of the week, and then finds that something else has come up so that the records cannot be taken care of.

The amount of paper work or reports you are responsible to do, compared to other pharmaceutical companies or sales organizations, is minimal. No one likes to be burdened down with reports—remember, for every report you submit, someone in the home office has to read and interpret. Consequently, the amount is limited to only pertinent information. However, paper work is a necessity and it's here to stay—so accept it. Without it no sales organization could function.

YOUR REGIONAL MANAGER

Your Regional Manager is the link between you, your Sales Manager, and the Home Office. He was promoted to an executive position from a territory because of certain attributes. He proved his sales ability with the doctor, the hospital, the technician, and with the various types of customers. He demonstrated his ability to think creatively. He is a teacher. He is the best friend you have. His principal job is to help you do a better job and make more money.

Your Regional Manager has a hard job. He always gives more than he receives—and does it willingly. When you run up against a difficult situation in your territory, such as a difficult buyer in your hospital or a physician who is hard to see, you can call on your Regional Manager. He, in most cases, can smooth out your problems because he has had similar situations in his own experience and solved them. He can help you to have a better conception of our products and their benefits.

While this man willingly gives of his time and experience, you should reciprocate by helping him. When he comes to travel with you, make him welcome. Take him to your good customers as well as the tough ones. He is your friend and should be treated as such. Give him a proper build-up when he is with you on a call. Don't say to the physician, "Dr. Smith, this is Bill Williams"; say rather, "Dr. Smith, this is my Regional Manager, Bill Williams." When someone is working with you, introduce him by name and title. The majority of physicians feel complimented to have a Regional Manager or home office management making the call with you. Take advantage of it. Take a selfish interest in your Regional Manager and get all you can out of him, but remember to reciprocate by being friendly, loyal, and cooperative.

ENTHUSIASM

The following are comments of different business leaders on Enthusiasm. But, before we go into their opinions, I know we all agree that Enthusiasm is contagious and you must have it to sell. Everyone has his own particular type of Enthusiasm from the loud desk-pounding type to the quiet sincere type. Enthusiasm, without question, should be sincere. Some of the factors that lend themselves to help pick up the inertia of Enthusiasm are Knowledge of the Product, Good Home or Family Relationship, Good Health, and Sincerity.

I'm not going to break these assets down one by one, I'll let you do that. Now to the letters.

"Enthusiasm based on knowledge produces a pleasing personality—one that begets confidence and inspires people to do what you have a right to expect of them. Life usually treats us about the way we treat others. If we act small, we can expect to be small with little influence on others. If we have a high respect for life and take an unselfish interest in others, we develop characteristics which make for genuine and sincere enthusiasm."

s/Don L. Jordan, Chairman of the Board
Johnson-Carper Furniture Co., Inc.

"Enthusiasm that is sincere and convincing is a salesman's most valuable asset—Genuine, contagious enthusiasm results from the proper blending of one's personality, pride, intellect, and emotion.

"Intellectually, enthusiasm results from an unquenchable curiosity and never-ceasing interest and knowledge. Without genuine interest in a product, for example, and complete knowledge of its qualities and its uses to the customer, no salesman can hope to be enthusiastic or to sell successfully. He would lack the basic elements.

"Emotionally, enthusiasm results from deep affection, devotion, and exertion. Through these our salesman demonstrates his conviction that his product is invaluable to the customer and, therefore, he can honestly, sincerely, and with pride identify himself with the product and his company."

s/Thomas B. McCabe, President
Scott Paper Company

"The most important factor in enthusiasm is SINCERITY and an earnest willingness to help others.

"Enthusiasm is not something you keep to yourself—it is contagious, it must be shared and built through use. You build what you use.

"As you give freely of yourself, enthusiastically serving others and making people glad you are around, your enthusiasm for life and for your work continues to increase. It is on this sincere type of enthusiasm that we build progressive organizations and strong and successful men."

       s/Maxey Jarman, Chairman of the Board
       General Shoe Corporation

"There are two kinds of enthusiasm:

  1. SUPERFICIAL ENTHUSIASM fools nobody, convinces nobody. It marks a man as being inept and insincere. It can do a salesman and his company more harm than good. It is phony enthusiasm.

  2. GENUINE ENTHUSIASM is both convincing and infectious. It stems from a thorough knowledge of the product or service a salesman is selling and of the buyer's needs and problems. It is a salesman's greatest asset—the one sure way to outsell competition and to build a secure future."

       s/J. C. Aspley, Chairman of the Board
       The Dartnell Corporation

ENTHUSIASM SELLS!

  1. ENTHUSIASM IS THE OUTWARD REFLECTION OF INNER BELIEF. It reflects our belief in ourselves, our company, our product or service. Hence it gives the doctor confidence in us and in what we offer.

  2. ENTHUSIASM REFLECTS KNOWLEDGE. The salesman who really knows just about all there is to know regarding his products radiates enthusiasm as naturally as a stove radiates heat. And prospects naturally prefer to do business with a salesman who knows the answers.

  3. ENTHUSIASM ENGENDERS ENERGY. And energy is the power that drives the salesman to make the calls which bring in the sales.

  4. ENTHUSIASM IS CONTAGIOUS. It enables us to override our fears and strengthens our ability to overcome doubts and fears in the minds of our prospects.

  5. ENTHUSIASM SELLS. It is the plus-value in the sales personality which makes the difference between the sales leaders and the also-rans."

       The Power of Enthusiasm in Selling
       By J. C. Aspley

WHAT YOU CAN DO TO SELL YOURSELF RICH:

1. Forget that you don't sell medical supplies. This chapter is worth the price of the book alone if it makes you remember you are selling advantages and benefits, not just a product.
2. Whatever product you represent, all you have to do is substitute your product wherever Mr. Johnson refers to his. His methods are priceless!
3. Don't ever try to sell again without using Bill Johnston's Product Analysis sheet; his F.A.B. sheet: Facts, Advantages, and Benefits; his P A C E S sheet: Performance, Appearance, Convenience, Economy, and Safety.

Very Useful Vignettes

Chapter 31

How you can use the following vignettes to make yourself a much better person in whatever you do.
1. The average egg
2. Shoplifting prevention
3. Your appearance
4. Copy the giants
5. How to handle a complaint
6. Don't call the boss
7. Welcome competition
8. Will you be ready when the company says...
9. Take the acid test

VIGNETTE NUMBER 1:
THE AVERAGE EGG

TO MANY PEOPLE, EGGS ARE EGGS. When you've seen one, you've seen them all. They are just that simple. Having seen one, it follows that you know all there is to know about eggs.

In a world where statistics are worshipped and the average is ideal, the egg is the paragon of conformity. Or is it?

What do we know about this egg? It looks like an ordinary egg. But do you know what a prairie owl's egg looks like? Come to think of it, is this egg sterile? If not, is the tick of life still in it?

If fertile, is it a male? If so, will it hatch? Into a Plymouth Rock? Or a Rhode Island Red? Or will it make a cupcake, an omelette, a jar of mayonnaise, or a salad sandwich?

Maybe an egg isn't much of a statistic after all. It only conforms on the surface. It can be counted, even candled, but not predicted, unless you know where it came from and watch where it goes. Therefore: next time you look at a statistic, think of the egg.*

*Young and Rubicam advertising agency ran this ad in the April issue of <u>Fortune</u> magazine in 1963.

I was able to take "The Average Egg" ad and use it in a sales presentation at Fedders national distributors sales meeting. At the end of the ad where it says "Next time you look at a statistic, think of the egg," I just changed it to, next time you decide to sell something to somebody, first buy an egg and then never forget that "look-alikes" don't always perform alike. I then continued on exactly as you would with your own product. I said, to many people, air conditioners are air conditioners. When you've seen one you've seen them all. It's just that simple. But NEMA (National Electrical Manufacturer's Association) says if an air conditioner has 6,000 BTU'S on the label it's like all other eggs—I mean air conditioners. But what happens if we look at the air conditioner as thoroughly as we looked at the egg? From there, I started to build on the hidden value of my product. It was a fresh approach to the old idea of talking about the hidden value in your product.

VIGNETTE NUMBER 2: SHOPLIFTING PREVENTION

Shoplifting prevention clinic! What in heaven's name could the subject possibly have to do with selling? That was my reaction. I went to the clinic with my wife who owns and runs a gift shop. The clinic covered all the bases of how and what to do regarding shoplifting. Then darned if the man in charge didn't start to talk about one of the best deterrents against shoplifters—good sales people. That's what he said. They don't have to have a gun or a badge, they just have to be doing a good job as a sales person. They don't form in little groups talking about what they did last night while somebody else is walking out with half the store. The speaker told how a good sales person has a good knowledge of the merchandise in his or her section; that if a sales person suspects a customer in his section of shoplifting, he should start straightening up things close to the person in question. "You keep that up long enough," the speaker said, "and you'll soon find out if you've got a shoplifter on your hands. A shoplifter will quietly leave."

So if you sell retail, sell right and you'll spare your company one of the biggest problems in todays retailing: SHOPLIFTING!

VIGNETTE NUMBER 3:
YOUR APPEARANCE

Your appearance has always been a factor, but today I believe it has taken on a new dimension. Not so long ago I had the pleasure of hearing a man speak on the subject of how you should look and act in front of your customers. He went over all the usual things you've been told, but came up with one that had the all male audience laughing their heads off. He said: "When you call on a customer and have long hair down to your shoulders, a droopy mustache and mutton chop sideburns, that customer may be looking at you and thinking, that S.O.B. looks just like my son, and I could kill him." You understand of course the reason the audience laughed so hard was because it dawned on them how true it was. I told the same thing to an audience I talked to about a month later and the sales manager wrote me to tell me that four of his men with crazy mustaches and long hair had done something about it. You might not like the idea of having to conform, and I don't think you should 100 percent, but tone it down. I've actually seen it affect a salesman's presentation.

I talked at a sales rally in Memphis where *Newsweek* magazine put on a show of how men should dress. They enlisted the help of all the local men's shops and had fat men, thin men, tall and short men model what they thought the well-dressed salesmen should wear. I've told a lot of men if there is any doubt in their mind about what kind of an outfit to buy to have a good total appearance, do what I do. Look in the window of a good men's shop. You'll see a gray, brown or blue suit displayed with the right shirt and tie, the right socks and shoes. When I find one I like I just go in the store and tell the clerk I want the whole outfit in whatever color I've picked in my size. I thought having pens and pencils sticking out of your jacket pocket went out with high button shoes, but I still see plenty of salesmen pushing water uphill. And remember, when you look smart, you feel smart and you'll find you'll sell better. You never get a second chance to make a good first impression.

VIGNETTE NUMBER 4:
COPY THE GIANTS

I'm one of the few fellows on the speaking circuit who couldn't care less how much you plagiarize anything you hear me say or write. In the name of the almighty, if you see somebody doing something better than you've been doing it, copy him. So few men take advantage of the idea. Wouldn't you copy Arnold Palmer if you could in golf? I keep telling all the little business men I talk to, to *copy the giants*. They became giants by doing more things right. Remember this quote from Woodrow Wilson: "I not only use all the brains I have, but all I can borrow."

VIGNETTE NUMBER 5:
HOW TO HANDLE A COMPLAINT

1. Ask the customer to tell you about it.
2. Listen (don't interrupt).
3. Repeat back, word for word, to the customer the facts as he has given them to you.
4. Express regret and be sincere about it.
5. Take action at once! Show him you intend to do something about his complaint and FOLLOW THROUGH!
6. Ask for more business, no hard feelings, and express the fact that you value his business and want more. (Sometimes as a result of a complaint a customer is lost because both parties are afraid to pick up where they left off.)

VIGNETTE NUMBER 6:
DON'T CALL THE BOSS

When you get the chance for the biggest sale you've ever made, DON'T CALL THE BOSS. I had the good fortune to work for a man by the name of Jake Sabitt who was the midwestern sales manager for Schenley Distillers. (At the time they were number 1 in the liquor industry.) Jake Sabitt was a legend in the liquor industry. He had made the largest sale of whiskey ever made, a million and a half dollars just after repeal. That'll give you some idea of how much money it would be today. He walked out of the offices of Charlie Walgreen with two cashier's checks, one for eight hundred thousand dollars and the other for seven hundred thousand dollars. Walgreen Drug Stores was the largest chain in Chicago. Jake told me that if he had called his boss when Mr. Walgreen started talking about a million and a half dollar order, he'd have blown the sale. He told me that all the brass would have descended on Mr. Walgreen, and pretty soon Mr. Walgreen would begin to wonder if he might just be making a mistake in ordering so much at one time. Jake closed by telling me that he made Mr. Walgreen feel that what he was doing was a very prudent move at that particular time. I always remembered what Jake told me. Once I sold an order for air conditioners to a tough-minded distributor, and for one fleeting second I thought maybe I ought to call my boss. Then Jake Sabitt's advice rang a bell. I showed this distributor how, if he placed a large order for air conditioners (and it was at the end of the season), he would be able to corner the market for next year. He bought it. I was glad I was right, and he was way ahead of his competition when the next season for air conditioning rolled around.

VIGNETTE NUMBER 7:
WELCOME COMPETITION

Many years ago I invented a toy plaque. One day I found myself talking to the top buyer for F. W. Woolworth. I don't know how it came about, but at one stage of the conversation the top buyer said to me, "Son, when we open one of our stores what we want is a Kresge on one side of us and one of the largest drug chain stores on the other."

For years I've listened to pathetic little businessmen ask if they could have my line exclusively. They'd be the only one in town. Then we could both die together.

I used to be the sales manager for the tape recorder division of Ampro Corporation. About five people in the country had a tape recorder at the time. It was a whole new idea. We advertised and worked hard at selling the idea to Mr. and Mrs. America. One day the president of the company called me into his office. He was really excited, but in the wrong way. He showed me a magazine for the photo industry that had a whole bunch of ads of companies that were now going into the tape recorder business. He was really shook up about all the competition we were going to have. I told him it came just in time, that so far we were trying to do it all by ourselves and not making much of a dent in the market. I was right and the president was wrong. A year later, with everybody in the act, we were on our way. If you ever have to pioneer a new product, pray for competition. It's the best help you'll ever get. Just one more shot: There is a place somewhere in New York

City that has block after block of electric motor and supply equipment companies—no stores in between; just a solid mass of places you can buy used and new electric motors. Nobody put a gun to any of their heads and told them they had to move right into a mine of competition. They did it because it pays off.

VIGNETTE NUMBER 8:
WILL YOU BE READY WHEN THE COMPANY SAYS...

Someday your company is going to quietly mention to you that they would like you to say a few words at the convention. You might be one of the salesmen who has been doing a good job or a district manager or a regional manager; you might be the head of the service department; you might be a buyer or an assistant buyer in a department store; or you might be one of the engineers in the plant. And they might just want you to explain to the sales department how the new saw is made and why the changes that have been made are a plus in its saleability.

Here is a splendid opportunity for you if you do a good job and present a good talk. But if your talk turns out to be a poor presentation, you could easily degrade a lot of the other hard work you have been doing. In heaven's name, don't ever let me hear you say after you blew it, "I wasn't hired to make speeches. I'm a salesman, an engineer, etc. etc. etc." Not in this world can you get away with that one. I've mentioned before in this book that I made every salesman who ever worked for me take the Dale Carnegie course. I also made them pay for it so I'd be sure they showed up. It's a priceless ingredient in the makeup of a successful man in today's world. Why the Dale Carnegie course? Simple, it makes you do something you won't take the trouble to do by yourself. It's the same with a health club. If we had any character we would never have to go to a health club to keep in condition. You can do it on the floor of your bedroom if you've got the character and stick-to-it-iveness.

Now if you can tell me you are going to be a slump all your life I won't badger you about learning how to get up in front of an audience and made a good speech. But all your life is a long time. You can't tell where you might end up. The trick is to be ready. For the fun of it, take a look at the fellows around you in your company, the ones they have asked to speak at some type of meeting. Are you as good as they? Someone once asked me how I learned to talk so well. I told him, by talking. I think I must have been really bad when I first started. But I stayed with it and found out the more I talked the better I got.

If you don't take this advice and still try to bull through a talk for the company with some notes and little homework, then be sure to read it. It is far better to read your talk than to deliver it badly through trying to memorize it. But remember, do your homework. What you put into it is what you'll take out—no more, no less.

VIGNETTE NUMBER 9:
TAKE THE ACID TEST

How much do you do each day to help yourself? Take your time, and be honest if it kills you.

Listed below are ten questions on ways to do a better job. I call it "THE BIG TEN." If you get any "no" answers, you're coasting. You won't have to worry about promotion, but you sure can worry about losing your job. It will just be a question of time.

1. Do you read and apply all the material the home office sends you?
2. Do you write down your plans, and constantly refer to them?
3. Do you ask your superior for help or criticism?
4. Do you read journals in your field to keep up with what is going on in your industry?
5. Do you analyze lost sales to learn what you might have done wrong?
6. Do you come to sales meetings with questions that you may be able to get the answer to from a fellow salesman or your boss?
7. Do you ask questions, provide answers, *take notes*, and otherwise participate actively in your sales meetings?
8. Do you practice your presentation outloud? And the same for your speech?
9. Do you write out all the objections you encounter, and work out good answers to them?
10. Do you ever write down the details of each big sale to see what they have in common?

Today Is the First Day of the Rest of Your Life

Chapter 32

---

1. Yesterday is history.
2. Habit! Read what you can do about it before you let another day become just a habit!

NEVER THOUGHT ABOUT THAT, DID YOU? It's not too late. Young or old, you can change your habits.

William James says:

Habit is a pleasure tool—it's a technique for simplifying your existence; for saving time and the energy of making decisions.

"Habit a second nature! Habit is ten times Nature," the Duke of Wellington is said to have exclaimed; and the degree to which this is true no one can probably appreciate as well as one who is a veteran soldier himself. The daily drill and the years of discipline end by fashioning a man completely over again, as to most of the possibilities of his conduct.

There is a story, which is credible enough, though it may not be true, of a practical joker. On seeing a discharged veteran carrying home his dinner, the joker suddenly called out, "Attention!" Whereupon the man instantly brought his hands down, and lost his mutton and potatoes in the gutter. The drill had been thorough, and its effects had become embodied in the man's nervous system.

Riderless cavalry horses at many a battle have been seen to come together and go through their customary evolutions at the sound of the bugle call. Most trained domestic animals, dogs and oxen, and omnibus and car horses seem to be like machines almost pure and simple, undoubtingly, unhesitatingly doing from minute to minute the duties they have been taught and giving no sign that the possibility of an alternative ever suggests itself to their mind.

Men grown old in prison have asked to be re-admitted after once being set free.

Habit is the enormous fly-wheel of society. It keeps the fisherman and the deck-hand at sea through the winter. It holds the miner in in his darkness and nails the farmer to his log cabin and lonely farm life through all the months of snow. It keeps different social strata from mixing. All this by habit. Already at the age of twenty-five you see the professional mannerism settling down on the young commercial traveler, on the young doctor, the young minister, on the young counsellor-at-law. You see the little lines of cleavage running through his character, the tricks of thought, the prejudices, the ways of the "shop," in a word, from which most of us can no more escape than his coat sleeve can suddenly fall into a new set of folds.

A man who broke me in as a salesman used to get out of the car, pulling the key out of the ignition with one hand while the other was reaching back of his seat for some point of sale material. He'd no more go into an account without that point of sale material than he would try to walk on water. He was the best salesman Schenley had in the Chicago office. He had just formed a good habit, and it paid off. The rest of the dummies would walk in empty-handed. You can guess how many ever walked back to where the car was parked and got some point of sale material.

They tell us the great thing in education is to make our nervous system our ally instead of our enemy.

All companies would be much better off if they could hire all their salesmen the day they finished college. There would still be time to train them in a better mold with better habits.

If you really want to correct some bad sales habits consider the things your company has asked you to do in the process of selling their product. As corny as it might seem, make a check list. Actually have a list made out that you check before you walk in to see a customer and then check it when you walk out. The day you start doing what I've just told you, you're in for the most pleasant surprise in your selling. If you followed your check list, it might look like this:

1. I completely covered our whole line.
2. I had our advertising program *with me*.
3. I had all the spec sheets *with me*.
4. I called for an appointment. I didn't barge in and hope the buyer would see me.

5. I knew what the account's inventory was.
6. I knew how much the account had purchased last year.
7. I've made a note of the buyer's complaint on a lost shipment of merchandise. Before my next call I'll check on it with the office and call the buyer back.

Well, you can fill in any of the other things that fit into the product or service you sell.

Remember I know as well as you those old *bad* habits are hard to break when you pass the twenty-five to thirty-year zone. But you can do it with my favorite word, PERSISTENCE!

TODAY IS THE FIRST DAY OF THE REST OF YOUR LIFE!

Sales Ideas

Salesmanship: He who works with his *hands* is a laborer. He who works with his *hands* and his *head* is a craftsman. He who works with his *hands*, his *head* and his *heart* is an artist. He who works with his *hands*, his *head*, his *heart* and his *feet* is a salesman.—Author Unknown.

One of the most common objections a salesman meets is—"It costs too much." Actually price ranks lower than . . . confidence in the wholesaler . . . style . . . quality . . . and service. For instance, why do you pay $100—$150 for a suit, instead of $50 for one at a bargain basement? You expect better quality, more service, more pleasure and greater usefulness. If price comes up as an objection, the customer usually is not sold. It is your cue to go over the vital points of your presentation again in an effort "to sell your customer away from price."— Bill Basinger, Henry V. Dick & Co., Charlotte, N.C.

Service begins when you open the customer's door. The sensible salesman does his level best to write the type of order that, in his judgment, will do the buyer the most good. The best order is the one that meets the buyer's requirements without overloading him. There is nothing that will wreck a buyer's relationship faster with a salesman than when he is sold more of a given product than he will ever need during a reasonable period.—"The Personal Satisfaction of Providing Service," by R. M. Sandell, Kar Products, Inc.

Build your reputation with your customers on honesty, integrity, product knowledge and truth. Handle his orders properly, keep errors to a minimum, meet required dates, avoid problems. If a problem presents itself, whether yours or not, try to solve it for him. See that he is billed properly, timely, and credits issued at once when due.—Don Montgomery, Moore Supply Co., Houston, Tex.

Compiled by National Candy Wholesaler

this information if it falls into our laps as opposed to going out after it with questions. For example, you can bet that if you're selling retail stores, those stores are going to be the first to know about a competitor. This is true of any business operation you are currently selling. It's no big problem to work this query into the conversation in an effort to learn if any new competitors have opened in the area. Such competitors immediately become potential customers.—*The American Salesman.*

The eager new product manager started on a swing around all divisions to talk about the new product and promotion plans. His first stop was Alaska, the most distant territory. His talk at the meeting of Alaskan salesmen reflected his enthusiasm for the new campaign. When he finally sat down he apologized to the territory manager for exceeding by a long way the time allocated for his speech. "No, not at all," said the territory manager reassuringly, "that was not too long at all. You merely shortened the winter for us."—*Sales Meetings.*

Enthusiasm is the opposite of boredom. Boredom tires—enthusiasm inspires. Boredom debilitates—enthusiasm exhilarates. Boredom vegetates—enthusiasm generates. Boredom stagnates—enthusiasm creates.—William Arthur Ward.

Most of us know that our present customers can be sources of information relative to ferreting out new customers. But do we put on a concerted effort to "milk" this information from our present people? There is a big difference in picking up

Index

A
Acid test, 201
Advertising, 37
Advertising agencies, 39-41
Appearance, 197
Aptitude—attitude, 19-21
Automotive sales and service, 115

B
Busy men have the time, 57
Buying decisions, 136
Buying motives, 133

C
Change—in the market, 159
Competition—it's healthy, 199
Complaints—how to handle, 198
Conforming—how to change, 127
Customer: don't judge his purchasing power by yours, 135
Customer relations, 71, 72
Customer value, 69

D
Distributor selling, 101

E
Education—how much, 83
Enthusiasm, 56, 149, 190, 191, 207

F
Factory representatives, 105
Farmer—practice what he does, 61, 63

G
Goethe, 53, 55

H
Habit, 203
How much can you make selling, 13, 14, 15

I
Image-makers, 33, 34
Insurance selling, 125
Invest in yourself, 43, 44, 45

J
Judge yourself, 29

K
Knowledge: how much do you have of your product, 58

L
Look alikes don't always perform alike, 195

M
Merchandising, 47, 48, 49, 50, 51
Mind, 25, 26
Motivation, 90
Mouse trap: did you build a better one, 158
Move up in class, 30

N
Names—remember them, 59
New products, 160

O
Objections—how to handle them, 181

P
Price, 156, 157, 206
Professional selling, 165 to 193

R
Rating: are you liked or disliked, 72
Real estate selling
Remembering what you've heard, 8
Retail selling, 95

S
Self-starter, 87, 88, 89, 90
Selling securities, 111
Service, 206
Shoplifting, 196
Shoppers—make them into buyers, 138
Silence, 57
Sincerity, 58
Smile, 59
Speech: how to make a good one, 131, 141, 153, 200
Success; 11, 163

T
Teamwork, 75, 76
Technical, 79, 80
Time, 65, 66, 67
Tools for your job, 4

V
Very useful vignettes, 195

W
Winner, 29